Isaac Leeser

Discourses on the Jewish Religion

Vol. IX, Third Series

Isaac Leeser

Discourses on the Jewish Religion
Vol. IX, Third Series

ISBN/EAN: 9783337138301

Printed in Europe, USA, Canada, Australia, Japan

Cover: Foto ©Lupo / pixelio.de

More available books at **www.hansebooks.com**

DISCOURSES

ON

THE JEWISH RELIGION.

BY

ISAAC LEESER.

הלוא כה דברי נאם ה' כאש וכפטיש יפוצץ סלע:
ירמ' כג' כט':

"BEHOLD! THUS IS MY WORD, SAITH THE LORD, LIKE THE FIRE,
AND LIKE THE HAMMER THAT SHIVERETH THE ROCK."

Jeremiah xxiii. 29.

VOL. IX.

THIRD SERIES.

PHILADELPHIA:
PRINTED FOR THE AUTHOR BY SHERMAN & CO.
5628.

Entered according to Act of Congress, in the year 1867,

BY ISAAC LEESER,

In the Clerk's Office of the District Court of the United States for the Eastern District of Pennsylvania.

STEREOTYPED BY SHERMAN & CO.

CONTENTS OF VOL. IX.

DISCOURSE	PAGE
I. The Testimony,	1
II. The Essence of Judaism,	27
III. True and False Worship,	41
IV. The Object of our Redemption,	57
V. The False Prophets,	73
VI. God Spoke,	100
VII. Our Consolation,	113
VIII. The House of the True God,	133
IX. The Israelite's Thanksgiving,	149
X. Israel and Civilization,	164
XI. The Law Tested,	177
XII. How to Mourn,	192
XIII. Revealed Truths,	208
XIV. Divine Charges,	226
XV. Our Strong City,	239
XVI. The 'Omer,	252

DISCOURSES

ON THE

JEWISH RELIGION.

DISCOURSE I.

THE TESTIMONY.*

MY FRIENDS!

Although we are not assembled this day in a house consecrated to God, still we have met for the purpose of doing honour to our Everlasting King, and to labour in his name. It has always been the custom of Israel, on all occasions of public assembly, not to let the words of prayer be wanting; it is הקול קול יעקב "The voice which is the voice of Jacob," which is ever acceptable on High; in this is our strength, in this our victory; herein angels of mercy join us to do honour to the Creator; and of this, in our deepest affliction, tyrants in all their power, nations in all their tumultuous wrath, could not rob us. Let us, then, not be unmindful of this our potent weapon,

---

* An Address, delivered at the schoolhouse of the Hebrew Education Society of Philadelphia, at the first opening of their school, on Sunday, the 4th of Nissan (April 6th, 1851).

the two-edged sword of God's praise which is in our mouth, and let us reverentially and with deep humility invoke the aid of our Father in heaven on the work which we are about to begin, in order that He may be with us at our first starting, and not withdraw from us his grace and aid till our task be accomplished.

O Lord Eternal! Thou hast commanded us in thy law, that we should propagate the doctrines Thou hast bestowed on us; since Thou hast ordained, "And ye shall teach them to your children, to speak of them when thou sittest in thy house, when thou walkest by the way, when thou liest down, and when thou risest up." It is in obedience to this behest that we, thy servants, have striven to establish a seminary where the children born unto Israel might be taught of thy laws, and acquire a knowledge of the sacred language of thy people, without being exposed to the danger of contamination, by instruction which is hostile to the faith which we derive from Thee. Long has our striving been in vain, our words fell on ears deaf to admonition; but at length, for which we bless thy Name, we are at the eve of commencing the work which is so necessary to the well-being of all descendants of Jacob. But, O! how feeble is this beginning —how small the number of those who have inscribed their names unto Thee; but we entreat Thee, do not despise the offering which we bring, unworthy though it be of thy acceptance; and cause it to prosper and flourish, since Thine is the power to bless and perfect what man begins in doubt and sorrow.

Long has thy Name been profaned among the gentiles, when they saw that they who were called thy people were untrue to their vocation, and faithless to the mission Thou hadst assigned them, to be a guide to the nations. The knowledge of thy word and thy ways has fearfully diminished, and many have fallen off, because they know not the principles of thy faith, and the duties incident to its followers. Grant then, O most merciful Father! that this school may become a shining light in Israel; that it may tend to invigorate with truth and knowledge the minds of many who otherwise would grope on their way in darkness; that its scholars may become quick in the spirit of salvation, and stand forth as Israelites in whom Thou art well pleased; and that through them many others may be drawn into the sacred influence, to devote to Thee their life, their best exertions, and their whole soul.

Upon the teachers, who are to engage in the holy work, send, we beseech Thee, thy gracious beneficence; inspire them with meekness, to labour in the arduous task which they have assumed, and with perseverance not to flag amidst discouraging trials to which they will be exposed. Lend eloquence to their tongues, and deep persuasion to their words, that they may be able to enchain the youthful hearts, and bind them indissolubly to thy service, so that in after-years they may rejoice over the multitudes they have brought under the overshadowing wings of thy Providence.

And upon us, and all the well-wishers of this institution, pour out the spirit of liberality and devotedness, that we may not be weary in our struggle, nor become faint-hearted, if immediate success crown not our enterprise. Yea, teach us to wait for thy aid, in meekness and submission, and not to expect too much from our own strength and our own endeavours; so that, persisting to work in the cause of thy religion, we may be strengthened with the hope that Thou wilt guide us aright, and make everything eventuate for the best, to the extension of thy kingdom, and the spread of thy glory, and the joy of the holy ones on earth, in whom Thou feelest delight. Be it thus thy will to establish the work of our hands, and to let thy beauty be revealed over us. Amen.

LADIES AND GENTLEMEN!

When Joshua, the successor of Moses, was nigh the end of his mortal career, he assembled the whole tribes of Israel at Shechem, and addressed the elders, captains, judges, and officers of justice, in a heart-stirring appeal, relative to their duties to their God, in reminding them how mercifully He had brought them and their fathers to be his servants. He left them, however, the choice of remaining faithful to the Lord, or selecting some of the various idolatries which were then in vogue, either that of the Mesopotamians, or of the Emorites, near whom they then dwelt; but whatever the people might resolve on, he declared his firm determination that he and his household would serve the Lord. The Israelites, however, who had been the witnesses of the mercy and might which had been displayed before them, had no doubt of the truth of their religion in their heart; they therefore chose the same worship which their leader had chosen, and they declared, "We also will serve the Lord; for he is our God." After again receiving an affirmation of this pious and prudent resolution, Joshua wrote all that had transpired in a book containing the law of God, and took a large stone and erected it there, under the beech tree which was near the sanctuary of the Lord; and then we read—

ויאמר יהושע הנה האבן הזאת תהיה בנו לעדה
כי היא שמעה את כל אמרי ה' אשר דבר עמנו
והיתה בכם לעדה פן תכחשון באלהיכם :

יהושע כד' כז' :

"And Joshua said, Behold this stone shall be as a testimony against us, for it hath heard all the sayings of the Lord which He hath spoken with us; and therefore shall it be as a testimony against you, that ye may not prove false to your God." Joshua xxiv. 27.

These last words of the son of Nun may appear strange to you, inasmuch as he ascribes hearing to an inanimate block of stone, and says that it shall be a testimony against those with whom he spoke. But it is not to be expected that Joshua meant to convey, or that the people understood him as implying, any such absurdity. It is only in a metaphorical sense that he spoke. The people had been assembled near where the stone lay on the ground, consequently all the words and promises which they uttered could have been heard by the stone had it been a living being; wherefore it might well be erected in that place, and remind all future comers, on seeing it, that on that very spot, and around it, their forefathers stood, when they solemnly declared that they would remain Israelites, and obedient to the words of God, though they had been offered the free choice of rejecting Him if they had preferred doing so; consequently the stone, by its silent presence, would be a testimony against the people, should they ever become untrue to their Liege-Lord, who had done for them so many wondrous and merciful deeds. It is well known to you how powerfully mementos of the departed affect us; how we can be made sad by recalling to mind some simple lay which we in infancy heard our mother sing; how we are constantly wrought upon by even trifling matters, which bring back before our memory events that we long since had deemed as faded and forgotten. It need not, therefore, surprise us that mankind, in all ages, have deemed monumental columns of high importance, as fixing historical events in the most energetic manner on the minds of the beholders; and it is only in obedience to a positive injunction, that the ancient Israelites did not invoke the aid of sculpture, or the other cognate branches of the plastic art, to commemorate their heroes and their beneficent exertions. The more reason was there for erecting simple, and if you will, rough stones, durable as they are, and almost bidding defiance to the all-devouring tooth of time, in order that they might serve to point out the spots consecrated by the occurrence of important events, which would then also call their attention to the fact that, because they were servants of the Incorporeal One, who cannot be represented by any outward figure, they had been interdicted to make any hewn images, the simplest of which had, in the corrupt taste of those times, been converted into objects of worship; wherefore the mere product of nature, unadorned and undefiled by the artist's chisel, must serve them, instead of the laboured monuments of Greece, Assyria, Babylon, and Egypt. Some would-be-wise men will, perhaps, esteem this prohibition of sculpture and carving as narrow and illiberal; but if we view the depravity and hero-worship consequent on representing the human figure in relief, as it was practised by the ancients—the consequent tendency of rising in imagination from the mortal to the Immortal, and to portray Him too with daring and impious hands—the means it gives to represent criminal acts and indecencies of all sorts, as we see but too often among moderns:—we need not feel any surprise that in our religion no opportunity was allowed to a prurient fancy so to degrade the highest moral good as to make it subservient to vice, or to elevate to an undue height frail mortality, and to invest it with attributes to which it has no claims. Besides all this, the emblematic pictures and sculptures of the ancients have long since lost their significance; and however some one highly endowed may yet be permitted to decipher their secrets, and the history and lessons they convey, it is not to be denied that, as guides to mankind, the stupendous works of antiquity are practically of no more use than the simple stone erected by Joshua.

You may say that, so far as permanence is concerned, the monument erected near the sanctuary at Shechem is no longer in existence; consequently, to us, at this late day, it is of no more use than the hieroglyphic-covered columns of Luxor and Karnac. True, most true; but it is precisely this perishableness of all structures, whether the rude or ornamental, which proves the utter fatuity of man when he vaunts that he is building for futurity. He may, indeed, pile up stone upon stone, wall on wall, but he has not secured his edifice from decay; nay, the very materials he employs, the hardest basalt and granite, will suffer from abrasion the moment after they are placed in rest. So, then, if even we know no more now the site on which Joshua raised his monument—it matters not; it spoke its instruction as long as it was required, whilst the mind of the people needed to be rekindled, whenever forgetfulness of God's word was threatened in the corruption of the times; but, brethren, though the stone itself has perished, and they have passed away, who, violating their pledge, suffered for the covenant broken, and the law violated: the object for which it was erected has not passed away, and the religion for which it was a testimony is as potent now as it was on that very day; and yet more, it is more firmly established in the hearts of all Israelites than at that early date of our history, when so many wavered and went often astray after strange gods who have no breath in their nostrils.

And let me ask you, What brings us here together this day? It is the very same idea which caused Joshua to set up his memorial stone,—it is to testify that we wish to erect an institution in honour of the name of God. The sanctuary is indeed no longer ours; we have only small places for meeting to pray and to exhort; and we lack the glorious manifestation of the Divine Presence which formerly animated and comforted us. But the law itself, which was to be glorified through means of the public ministration of the priesthood, is not yet extinct, and claims of us, no less than in days of old, that we should spread it among all classes, as we read: "Assemble together the people, the men, and the women, and the children, and thy stranger who is within thy gates, in order that they may hear, in order that they may learn, and fear the Lord your God, and observe to do all the words of this law." (Deut. xxxi. 12.) Our law was not only given for the rich, the learned, the wise, the aged, the native born, the noble, and the priest, but for all who bear God's soul in their bosom, —it was bestowed as the inheritance of all mankind; wherefore all who were within reach of instruction were to be assembled to take part in the septennial ceremony of its public proclamation by the political chief of the people, in order that all might be animated by one desire to learn how to obey the will of the universal God, to whom all on earth bear the relation of children to their Father, of scholars to their Teacher. And we have come hither to-day to commence a school of instruction, open alike to the poor and the rich, the Israelite and the stranger, where it shall be the principal business of the teachers to imbue the mind early with true conceptions of the Godhead, and to repeat the lesson so frequently, by a daily putting line upon line and precept upon precept, that Judaism may become a part of the very nature of our pupils, without which they will not be able to exist, even if they should at a future day be tempted to cast it off for the glare and allurement of the hostile world beyond. It is not an easy thing, though some of you, my hearers, may think otherwise, to acquire this staunch love for religion; or else why do we see so many violations of its precepts daily and hourly practised before our eyes? Had Israelites that devotion which they ought to have, they could not so disregard their duties. It is education only which can correct this, and a constant exhorting at home and at school which can result in a God-fearing conduct through life. You may ask me, "Are there not many highly educated who are unfaithful? not many ignorant who are pious?" I readily answer "Yes," to both these questions. But though you do find the ignorant pious after their fashion, as *far as they know how*, and the learned often desperately wicked, this does not gainsay that true piety and an enlightened zeal are only found in those who have been inly tinctured with divine wisdom. For who were the great leaders of our race at all times? were they the unlettered? Who were the prophets? were they the uninstructed? Who were the most glorious martyrs? were they the ignorant? No, fellow-Israelites, they were all, whether men or women, those in whom the spirit of knowledge dwelt, and it was in their footsteps that the multitudes followed, whether they made their pilgrimage to the temple at Jerusalem, whether they ranged themselves under their country's banner on the day of strife, although they knew that all efforts would be in vain, since the enemy had penetrated within their walls, or whether they hastened to a yet more glorious death when tyrants demanded their blood as the price of maintaining their religion.

We in our day require the same devoted zeal among our household, in order that we may maintain the proper influence over its members. All Israel may in truth be viewed as one large family, in which each one has assigned a part which he must achieve, or be recreant to his trust. But, alas! how many have proved so! look at the records of the congregations in this country, and you will seek in vain for the representatives of many families among the professing Jews. Some have died out by the want of male descendants to bear their names; but many others have left the synagogue, either by apostacy or the quiet intermingling with the gentiles; and in addition to several families thus extinct already, others are fast hastening to the same deplorable state. Have you ever reflected on this fact? I have, many, many times, with a heaviness of heart which I cannot describe to you. To see the names once honourable among Israel borne by those, who are in feeling the bitterest opponents of our race, and the more so because they know, themselves, that they are ours by the father's or mother's side, is indeed a cause of the deepest grief to a sincere follower of the God of Jacob. And I ask you again, Have you never reflected on this fact? If you have, you must have discovered that nearly all such connexions have resulted from one cause, that is, that the offending parties did not consider Jewish families good enough for them to associate with; they regarded themselves a degree higher than all the Hebrews they knew; and hence they sought for alliances where they fancied their noble blood would suffer no contamination. You may think that I speak harshly; but does the fact bear me out? does your own experience confirm what I say? I appeal to yourselves, and let me be condemned, if in your innermost souls you find not a response only too affirmative to my words. It is nothing to the matter that persons of all grades of society have so offended; for, alas! it requires neither wealth, nor intellect, nor station, to puff up the human heart with pride, and no one is so mean but he is in his own conceit higher than all the people in importance. There have been others lost to us, because they felt themselves neglected by other Israelites, they were not appreciated as they deserved; so they thought, and they threw themselves into the arms of those who are always anxious to receive those straying from the Jewish flock. But whence arose this self-assumed superiority on the one side and the degradation on the other? Do you know this? Only reflect a moment, and the matter will become clear to you. Answer me, Where were our religious schools in former times? where are they now? It has always been to me a subject of profound astonishment and deep regret, that there was not a single school all over the country, until very lately, where a Jewish child could obtain any information on his religion. The synagogue was no place for instruction, because public lectures formed no part of the exercises. Family-worship, except in rare instances, was unknown, and family religious reading was not thought of, beyond a perusal of the Bible in the common translation, which was first ordered to be read in churches by authority of King James the First of England. The religious books accessible were limited to the works of the late David Levi, who in his lifetime was but ill-rewarded for the strenuous exertions he made in the cause of Judaism. Our Jewish predecessors in this country had only one place of meeting, and this was the synagogue where the worship was uniformly the same every Sabbath in the year, the tunes only varying to suit the various occasions for which they are very happily adapted. Could such a system tend to make men and women familiar with their faith? could it produce a fusion of wills and a harmony of souls, not to speak among natives and foreigners, but among the natives themselves? It is idle to expect it, for many knew not a word of Hebrew; the language of their worship was an unknown tongue to them; consequently the sounds, beyond the sweetness of the melody, fell like an unmeaning noise on their ears, and no improvement, no lifting up of the heart could be expected. And where a little Hebrew was acquired from some casual travelling teacher, it served more to deepen the shadow of the absence of information, than to remove it, just as the taper reveals to us more grimly the desolation and darkness of a subterranean prison, the outlines of which are not to be discerned by the flickering flame which we carry in our hands.

It was indeed surprising that so many years should elapse without due efforts being made to establish schools, and place the worship in the synagogue on a better footing. But though the evil was so apparent, it was allowed to continue unchecked, until the eyes of many were painfully opened to the want of love and harmony existing among us. People who had not in youth any familiar intercourse, who had been exclusively reared among gentiles, who had no friends among their own nation, could not sympathize with the other Israelites, who moved in a different or inferior station to themselves. The sequel was estrangement from religion, and a constantly decreasing obervance of the precepts of the Bible. I was told by an aged gentleman, now no more, that about seventy years ago a Jewish woman, who kept a boarding-house in New York, was remiss in some small observance which I have forgotten. The trustees of the synagogue, on learning this, at once proclaimed her house forbidden, and enjoined on all to abstain from eating with her at her table; and only upon a reparation of the wrong was the interdict removed. You may say that this was tyranny, an unwarranted interference in private family-matters; I cannot agree with you in such an opinion, as it was a public affair in which the pious synagogue-elders thought themselves authorized by custom and prescriptive right to interfere. But be this as it may, it shows the high degree of conformity then prevailing in the oldest congregation in the country. Now look at the contrast with the present state of affairs! See how many violate the Sabbath; how many are married out of the pale of Judaism; how many eat forbidden food; how many disregard the Passover; how many neglect the precept of circumcision, and then say, that we have not changed for the worse.

 I said the evil had become so apparent, and that something was necessary to be done, that a friend of Israel, a friend* of mankind, thirteen years ago undertook, unsolicited and of her own accord, to open a place of instruction for one day in the week to all who might choose to avail themselves of its advantages. The school was begun with hardly any books suitable for the purpose; and now behold! we have a good though a small series, every way calculated to serve the end in view, as the works embracing it convey a rational account of our religion, both its theory and practice, and tend powerfully to make a lasting impression on the youthful mind. I cannot doubt that much good has already resulted from it. Friend-

---

* Miss Rebecca Gratz.

ships have been cemented which probably will last during life; children have learned to know each other as Israelites, and to admire each other's character, who under other circumstances would never have come in contact; and I have every reason for believing that evil and anti-Jewish influences have been eradicated from the minds of some who otherwise might have forsaken our communion. I do not stand, however, here to flatter or to blame unduly: I have been asked by my colleagues to urge the importance of our enterprise. Therefore permit that I point out the defects of a mere Sunday-school, unaided by any other seminary. I will again acknowledge, before I proceed farther, that the example of the benevolent lady, whom we all esteem, and whom I am proud to be permitted to call my friend, and that of her disinterested assistants, has been imitated in various other parts of the country, until the just charge of actual ignorance is no longer applicable to all places where this has been done. But no one can say, that much has been accomplished towards diffusing a knowledge of the language of the Scriptures, without which no education of an Israelite can be complete. The little that can be acquired in extra hours, when the children have not to recite their usual lessons or to study them, is not enough, and must necessarily be very inefficient. The child is wearied with conning over matters which are in themselves of but questionable use, even when thoroughly acquired; and when you demand of him now to repair to his Hebrew teacher, he will find out a thousand reasons for desiring to escape from this unwelcome additional task. And I tell you, without in the least qualifying my assertion, that without an adequate knowledge of the Hebrew, sufficient at least to understand the Scriptures and the ordinary prayers, no Israelite can allege that he has acquired that knowledge which is all in all to him. A Hebrew not to be a *Hebrew in language*, when this is within his reach, is an absurdity, and it requires no argument to prove this proposition. And pray, why should we not teach to all our children the holy tongue, that they may be able to speak understandingly of God's word when they sit at home, and when they walk together by the way? Few are acquainted with the rich treasures of our literature; and now, when modern investigation is throwing so much light on this, no less than other subjects, it sounds strangely that to English and American Jews the whole is perfectly inaccessible.

Well may I ask you again, Shall this be always so? will you be always satisfied with things as they are, when you see the evil that has already resulted to our communities from this want of education? Our Society, however, has made it its object to become, if permitted by you, and if duly encouraged, under the blessing of Heaven, to whose safe keeping we commit it, an earnest agent to remove the reproach so far as our sphere of action can extend. We purpose to combine elementary and afterwards scientific education with a gradual and progressive acquirement of Hebrew, Hebrew literature, and religion. It is not to be as in other schools, a secondary matter whether the children learn Hebrew and religion or not, but they are to acquire these, if even nothing else can be imparted. Still imagine not that we are not fully alive to the importance of classical and elegant literature; we know how to appreciate both, and we trust that in a year hence our teachers will prove to you that Jewish children can advance in all the necessary branches of education under the superintendence of instructors of their own people no less than of others. We mean, however, to let the objects and concerns of eternal life not be merely the work of spare-time and a leisure-day, but to see that daily, and in the usual school-hours, the language and religion of our fathers are properly and fully illustrated. Permit me to call your attention to one fact: The members of the committee of school-directors, with a single exception, have no offspring of their own old enough to be participants in the benefit which the school is to confer; it is merely a sense of duty which impels them to be active in the cause, and to incur, if need be, a considerable amount of labour to carry out their views. But as this is the case, the greater obligation rests upon those who have children, and who wish to rear them in a religious and hopeful manner, to send them to us, that we may fulfil in them the duty which in obedience to our religion we have assumed.

But, I hear some one say, What guarantee can you give us that, when we remove our children from other schools, they will be properly taught the branches of a good general education? And it is, I apprehend, precisely this fear which has hitherto withholden many of you from entering your children as scholars on our books. But let me tell you that this is not wise, though it may be prudent. Our efforts must fail, if we meet with no encouragement; this I am willing to acknowledge; but, on the other hand, I maintain that we shall do more than redeem our promise, if the children are intrusted to our care. What is to prevent us giving as good an education as is furnished in public or private schools? do you believe that we cannot teach reading, writing, arithmetic, history, geography, and the higher branches, if these be required? The very idea is absurd; whatever the scholars show an aptness for can be taught as well, to say the least, under Jewish supervision as any other. Only try us, if it be only for one year; and if at its expiration you are dissatisfied with the progress of your children, taking as the standard of comparison what they have acquired elsewhere before, we shall be willing to acknowledge that we have failed.

You must, however, reflect again, that we do not merely charge ourselves with simple education; we wish to return your children to you at the end of each season improved in manners and morals. We wish to subject their minds to a wholesome restraint, where love shall govern and not force, where intellect is to lead, not vain ambition. Look at the effects of the Sunday-school, how they have ennobled natures, some thought incapable of improvement: and then say that the effect will not be much greater if the discipline be carried out through the whole period during which children are at school. It will of course take some time to get things in a proper train; perhaps several weeks must elapse before we can fairly assert that we have made a proper beginning; the thing is yet new, and circumstances, the surest indications of Providence, must show how we are to proceed; only have a little patience, the same that you would demand if you all were in our place, and we promise that we will faithfully strive to do our whole duty. It is possible also, that we may commit some mistakes at the very outset and during the subsequent existence of our enterprise; but shall this deprive us of your confidence? We trust not; we are all working in one cause; parents, teachers, managers, children, have all one object, that is, the diffusion of a knowledge of our religion; and hence we hope that any error which may be discovered shall be pointed out to us with candour and mildness, and we will endeavour to amend, so far as this may be practicable with the means and materials at our disposal. Only let me beg you, not to doubt hastily of a good result; it has been well said that "our doubts are traitors;" and it is certain that no great enterprise ever succeeded where the actors themselves doubted of their final success. To insure a happy issue we must have but one thing in view, namely, the *end* we are aiming at; we must not regard great or small obstacles as things worth minding, but move straight onward, and let each step taken in advance be the forerunner and guarantee of the next succeeding one. Believe me, that the greatest results are obtained by slow and continuous minor advances; and they succeed the best who persevere the longest, without despairing of their chances of carrying out what they at first dimly conceived to be within the range of their possibility. As little as wealth or renown is suddenly acquired, except in rare instances, can any enterprise, whatever it be, expect to prove itself at once among the events which are established in the full tide of success. Therefore I tell you, demand not of us that we shall accomplish impossibilities all at once; that we are to gather in this institution children of various stages of intellect and progress in domestic education, and mould them without delay into scholars of a uniform conduct and progress. Without a miracle, this will be impossible, and we are not vain or foolish enough to claim the ability to accomplish the impracticable. But let me beg of you all, not to undervalue our and your capacity for succeeding with this school, because we are Jews. The remark is often made, that we Israelites cannot do things like other people, and that we are altogether too self-willed to succeed where others find no bar to carry out their views. For my part I will never believe that we are inferior to the best of mankind in whatever we devote our attention to. Look at the great progress we have made in commerce and the mechanic arts wherever we had a fair field of action: and I see no reason why the same result is not equally certain in every pursuit to which we may seriously devote our energies. It is and has been our misfortune for many centuries, that small trading, and at best large commerce, has been our main pursuit; still, with all the disadvantages of our position, we have maintained a high character as an educated and intellectual people, though at times our educational systems have been highly defective. But I ask you, what is to prevent us in this free country, where all legal disqualifications are unknown, from advancing with the same or greater rapidity in intellectual pursuits with our fellow-citizens of other persuasions? What a humiliating confession would it be, were we to acknowledge that we did not establish religious schools, because we lacked the capacity and energy to undertake them, though we had ample means and a fair opportunity to do so. Away with such croaking! let us not hear the ominous sounds, "We cannot." We can, we must, we will! say this all of you, induce others to say the same, and then you will soon see whether Israelites can succeed in disseminating education and religious knowledge as successfully as the best and most enlightened denomination, whatever this may be.

I use plain language, I deal in no flowers of oratory, and I trust, therefore, that I shall be best understood. It is not so much to the feelings that I wish to appeal as to your good judgment, and hence I hope that you will not get impatient when my address detains you longer than you expected. The subject is one of the highest importance, and concerns you all, my hearers, whether you are rich or poor. Could I have the opportunity of seeing you here frequently, I might indeed cut my remarks short to resume them at another time; but as this may perhaps never be in my power, I must crave your indulgence to some few other considerations in connexion with the subject.— To Israelites their religion is no *luxury*, excuse me for using so strange an expression, but a matter of primary importance. An Episcopalian need not be a high or low churchman in order to believe in his system; for he has a wide range in which to move; and he can be a Nazarene, and for all we know fully as good as any in his sect, though he turn Baptist or Quaker. But a Jew is no Jew if he has not a firm hold on his peculiar opinions and distinguishing practice. Theoretical Jews can exist; we have, unfortunately, many such; but they are not the Israelites of the Scriptures, because the material element of this character, *religious conformity*, is absent. We know, moreover, no exemption from duty; we have no standard of indulgences or restrictions; no noble classes who may transgress, no lower orders who may yield themselves to degrading vices in order to gratify the sensualities of the lordlings, who look upon them with contempt even whilst they minister to their pleasures. The Jew is a Jew, whether he is the peddler that bends double under the burden which his laborious shoulders carry, or the baron of the Austrian Empire who idles away his hours on the luxurious sofa. The hopes of the last are not a whit higher and nobler than those of the first, and this one has the same claims to immortality and a glorious hereafter, as the most favoured child of luxury. Fortune's gifts may be, by the will of Providence, very unequally distributed; but let not their possessors deem themselves better men or more God-favoured on this account. They have a tangible advantage in their exemption from toil; they may lie down at night without torturing their brain how to provide for their little ones by the dawn of to-morrow. Is not this enough for them? must they also wish to perpetuate for their families a rank which the now humble and their offspring are never to attain? Weak! silly! wicked idea! *God* has elevated you, I tell you, not *you* have acquired your position by your unaided skill and labour; and He can unmake you, bring you down again to the dunghill whence you sprung, or your children, should you even be carried on a splendid bier to the grave, may have to claim the assistance of those whom you despise as too inferior to associate with you and yours. The world, and especially this country, presents so many instances of changes of fortune, that it would be superfluous for me to hunt for examples of which you, my hearers, know many in your own experience. Let us hope, therefore, that no silly pride will prevent parents of all standings in society from availing themselves of the advantages which we hope to offer to you. "Ho! let all you who are thirsty," says the prophet, "come to the waters, and he too who hath no money; come ye, buy and eat; yea, come, buy without money and without price wine and milk." The word of God is free to all, it is the water, the bread, the wine and milk of life; it refreshes, it satisfies, it rejoices, it nourishes. It is given to all, offered to all; and we summon all within our reach, as did the ancient prophet, to partake of the repast which we hope to spread for you in the name and by the aid of God. We demand of those able to pay, a small fee towards defraying the expenses which we have to incur, and we trust that this will be cheerfully given; but they who are not blessed with a superabundance of means are invited, nevertheless, to intrust to us their children, and we promise them that they shall not suffer the least reproof for the inability of their parents. All we ask of them is to send their children tidily dressed, and cleanly in their persons, so that no stain will attach to them for their humble state. And let me here remark at once, that nothing so promotes good conduct and proficiency in study as scrupulous cleanliness; in a dirty body a dirty soul too often dwells, and the exterior is mostly a fair index of the inward man. Cleanliness, say our wise men, is the first step to the acquisition of holiness, and it is a necessary element of Jewish life, as our holy law amply proves. It is not to be questioned that, if the children of the poor come hither so that all can freely associate with them, it will be an incentive for the rich to apply to us also to take their offspring under our charge; and only the non-observance of this rule can operate as an excuse to withhold any one from taking advantage of the institution we now commence.

Let no one think that any injury can result to better trained children, by associating with those not so fortunate as themselves; in after-life they will have to meet with persons of all classes, and it is no detriment that they become early acquainted with the fact that all are not prosperous alike. It will produce in them kindliness of feeling, at finding that the same virtues can dwell in a heart covered by a frieze coat, as that which beats under a velvet mantle, and that the sorrows of the poor are the same as those of the rich. This is *levelling upward;* you elevate the character of the humble, by bringing them in contact with those of better manners and greater refinement; and with children of good religious character, you need not fear that they will corrupt yours, whilst they acquire from them politeness and good breeding. This is well understood in the country where I was born. Universal education has long since been established there; and at the same colleges where the sons of the nobles acquire their collegiate education, the children of the day-labourers are freely admitted. The former have to pay the annual stipend which the rules require, whilst the others enjoy precisely the same advantages and privileges without any charge whatever; and it is not rare that the poorest excel the others in every requisite of intellect, industry, and aptness for study. But what need is there to go over the ocean to seek for examples of the kind? Look at your own great statesmen, your Clay, your Webster, your Fillmore, and thousands of others, and they were the children of poverty, of the unknown. And who dares now to remind them of their origin? They have their title of nobility from nature's God, and show me the worldling who would dispute this claim, valid as it is above all others.

But much as I have yet to say, I find that it is time to close. It has been my endeavour to exhibit to you, in as condensed a manner as possible, the necessity of our school, its practicability, and the happy effects it may produce, if it is rightly encouraged. Its friends and projectors have laboured long to bring it so far as to make a commencement; doubts and difficulties have surrounded every step in advance we have taken, and much labour and kindness will be required to keep it in operation. It is our intention, should the demand make it necessary, and our funds suffice, to open district-schools at convenient distances, so as to afford all children an opportunity to avail themselves of our Hebrew education. For the present we have selected this place* as the most central, and we hope that no captious fault-finding will prevent all our space to be soon claimed by attentive scholars. The committee of school-directors pledge themselves to do all in their power to afford the utmost satisfaction, and to act in all cases with strict impartiality.

---

* Phœnix Hall, Zane (or Filbert) Street above Seventh, not far from Market Street.

In conclusion, permit me, like Joshua of old, to call your attention to this stone, as it were, in the great building of righteousness, on which all Israel should labour, which we have just set up. It is a testimony against you, O Israelites of Philadelphia! whether or not you are true to the Lord your God. Cherish it, labour that it may become a chief cornerstone in an extended system of education, whence future teachers and ministers of Israel may go forth, to propagate the word of God: and you will have performed your duty, a duty which is incumbent on you and all our brothers wherever they are. Neglect it, and you will have perhaps to deplore apostacy in your own family, and a public desecration of the Name of God by some of your offspring, whom you would sooner follow to the grave, than see them thus dishonour you and your faith. It is for your own sakes that we call on you to aid us in our effort; you will rejoice when you see those dear to you intelligent servants of God, and familiar with his word, being thus faithful from knowledge and not mere conformity by descent. You never, we trust, will regret the exertions and outlay you have made in this cause; and they who have laboured to bring the Education Society into existence, under the blessing of Providence, will deem themselves amply compensated, when they see that their striving has in part brought "peace on Israel."

Nissan 4th. } 5611.
April 6th.

DISCOURSE II.

THE ESSENCE OF JUDAISM.*

To the God of Israel, the Father of all creatures, the Lord of all spirits, be praise and glory, from the rising of the sun to his setting, from all the children of man, whom his power has called into life, now and forever. Amen.

Brethren!

Having been invited by your Board of Managers to deliver an address on this Sabbath in your synagogue, I know of no more fitting subject on which to descant than the general tendency of that religion which we all profess in common, whether we are of the German or Portuguese mode of worship, or whether we first saw the light in America or in any of the various divisions of the old world. We are all Israelites, are either by descent or by adoption sons of Jacob, and no one is exempt from a due obedience to the law which is the outward token of our faith, and no one, on the other side, can be said to have duties to perform, if we take the general mass, which are not equally incumbent on all others. There are indeed different orders, such as priests, judges, superintendents of public affairs, and teachers of religion,

---

* A sermon for Sabbath Kedoshim, spoken in the Synagogue Rodef Sholem, Philadelphia.

to whom peculiar obligations are assigned; but these affect not their general obedience; and the especial acts required of them extend only to the general good, for the furtherance of which the various selected classes have needs to be established; since neither an Aaron, nor a David, nor a Samuel, nor an Isaiah, was selected in order to glorify himself; and whatever either or all of these were called upon to execute, was merely to fortify the large masses of their countrymen in the observance of the precepts in which all had a common interest. But as respects pure morality and the relative obligations which each man has to the other, there was not, and could not be any difference in the different ranks of society, inasmuch as all had the same Chief to follow, and all owed obedience and implicit fealty to the same God, who declared all alike to be his children.

Let us now take as the text of our reflection of to-day the following verse from this day's Sidrah,

את שבתתי תשמרו ומקדשי תיראו אני ה' :
ויקרא י״ט ל׳ :

"My Sabbath shall ye observe, and my sanctuary shall ye reverence: I am the Lord." Lev. xix. 30.

All duty is, according to the true principles of Judaism, referable to one single cause, and this is the will of God as revealed to us in his word. You cannot indicate to me a single act which is obligatory upon us that is not contained in or at least derived from the Scriptures; and if it be possible to point out any not so authenticated, we may at once say that its execution is a voluntary act on our part, but is no obligation, for the infraction of which we are punishable, and for the observance of which on the other hand we are entitled to reward. Punishment and reward are properly applicable to duty only; we are ordered by God to fulfil certain precepts, some of which are easy and others difficult of execution, and the measure of our disobedience or obedience fixes our liability to divine and civil visitation for our acts, or exhibits us as entitled to commendation from God and our fellow-men, and the consequent happy and gratifying results springing from this state of things. It is according to this view that we are simply bound to become acquainted with the principles of the revealed religion, which we justly assume to be from God, in order that we may know what acts to do and what others there are which we must avoid; and the closer any one of us approaches the standard thus discovered, the nearer will he be perfect, so far as this is practicable for us to become. At best will this perfection be exceedingly difficult for us to acquire; we are so surrounded with temptations, we are so constantly imagining that we are excused by circumstances for failing in our duty and faltering in our path, that we must often feel shame and contrition at discovering how easily we have been lured away to do that which we would condemn in others, if we observed them guilty of the same faults; and yet how little do we struggle before we yield to allurement, how glad indeed are we to have so paltry an apology, as an opportune and convenient temptation to do what is wrong. This is our course even when we know our line of duty: how much more then must we be exposed to evil deeds, should we be absolutely

3*

ignorant of the source whence it is derived! You have heard, no doubt, a great deal said of the innocence of man in a state of nature, by which is meant that state of lawlessness, where he roams about at will without moral or civil restraints, indulging in all imaginable fancies which his own impulses may direct him to. Without entering deeply into the inquiry whether such a state ever can exist, even amongst the most savage tribes, it must at once strike you, that the unrestrained license in one must operate to the injury of all others; for it is not to be supposed that, when a man is absolutely free to do as he pleases, he will be restrained from any act of aggression upon the person and property of others, if he deems such a trespass, as we view it in our state of civilization, conducive to his pleasure and within the limits of his strength to accomplish.

Nature, we may be sure, is as strong in one as in another; the desire for gratification and to possess is powerful in all alike. If, therefore, there be no law to restrain the impulse to have and to enjoy, there can be no peace, no property, no love, no rights; but all would be one universal scene of warfare, anarchy, hate, and plunder; the strong would override the weak, and the latter would plan secret and cunning devices to accomplish by craft what he lacks in brute force, to be revenged on the other. Consequently if you abolish *law*, you abolish civilized society; for if even you might succeed by any, the barest, possibility to enable a savage to live alone in the recesses of a mountain-fastness, or the solitude of the forest unrestrained and uncontrolled, you cannot give him a single companion, not to mention many, without establishing at once a system of reciprocal rights and duties. No one can submit unconditionally to the will of another and be happy or even negatively content; he will sigh to be released from the bonds of such depressing slavery; he will want to know how far the bounds of the power of his tyrant extends; and if he can find none, he will not rest till he has discovered some method to set a limit to the will that oppresses him, so that he may tell him, "Thus far shalt thou go, but approach nearer at thy peril."

So far, therefore, is the law of God from abridging our natural rights; so far is it from destroying our independence; so little does it deprive us of the least that we could claim as justly our due: that it is at once the exponent of our rights, and the best definer of our duties; since it marks out what we must do to others and what we have an undoubted right to require from them. All just legislation must be a system of checks and balances; something must be granted in return for every demand; there must be relaxation for every exertion, there must be an indulgence for every sacrifice required, and so on the other hand there must be no reward without toil, no glory without previous merit. Our wise men have an expression which exhibits this idea in a simple light: כי שלא טרח בערב שבת מה יאכל בשבת "If one has not laboured on the eve of the Sabbath, what shall he eat on the Sabbath?" meaning, since it is not permitted to labour on the day devoted to rest to dress our food, no one can justly partake of a meal, if he has it not in readiness on the day of preparation which precedes it. So also can man expect no reward without he has deserved it; no rest if he has not toiled for it; no renown if he has squandered away the precious hours; no tranquillity of soul if he has not subdued his evil inclinations in deference to the demands of religion. It is accordingly not so much the gratification of a desire to rule uncircumscribed in the world, which induced our gracious and heavenly Father to bestow on us his law, as the knowledge He had of our fallible nature that we required a guide, sure and unwavering, which is to point out to us whatever we should do or avoid; which should teach us when we should aid our neighbour, and when to expect his support; when we should bestow gifts, and when we may look forward to receive them; when we should offer consolation, and when we should be entitled to have the sympathy of others bestowed on us; and we may be sure, that mankind will be then in the greatest state of peace and prosperity, when the fewest possible have cause to complain of the acts of oppression committed and of the deeds of charity denied them by others. And O! how happily might our life glide away, if each would look upon the other as his friend, whom he is bound to love and whom he is willing to cherish as one equal with him in the eyes of the Creator; if the strong would rejoice in his strength to assist the weak against his oppressor; if the rich would look with pleasure upon his wealth when it enables him to open wide his hand to the needy one, his brother; when the wise would glory in his wisdom at the moment he steps abroad to diffuse the cheering light of truth and science, among those whom his words may lead to a better appreciation of life and duty; and when those who are humble would not need to fear to lay their distress open to the attentive ear of their loving neighbours; when innocence might freely claim the arm of power for its protection; poverty appeal without dread of refusal to those who have enough of life's abundant store; and when the simple might frankly ask for instruction and it not be denied to them. But alas! how sad is the reality around us; there is indeed much that is heavenly scattered all over the earth; there are brothers and sisters of the needy, there are those in whose houses the poor find a cheerful welcome, to whom it is enough that a fellow-being suffers, to excite their warmest pity, as they hope to be heard in their hour of distress; but there are many who can see unmoved the tears of the orphan, and turn away unpityingly from the streaming eyes of the lonely widow; to whom the groaning of the captive is sweet music, and who glory over innocence ensnared and inexperience steeped by them into the whirlpool of crime. And yet such as these are often called the great ones of the earth; they are raised high amidst those who have power, and many call them the illustrious of mankind; the glittering star of proud rank graces their bosom, and historians love to record their deeds, and sycophants flatter them by saying that in men so exalted *that* is venial sin, a slight transgression, which is degrading crime and low debauchery in the humble.

Do you now wonder that the divine legislation, which is ours, endeavoured to place, and succeeded in so doing, all human beings on one level of obedience to a superior law and subjection to one Supreme Being? Assuredly not; for however low any one may stand in the ranks of society, he feels in himself the spirit divine which animates the most exalted; he sees that they must eat, if even more dainty food than satisfies him, of the products of the earth which he cultivates in the broiling heat, whilst the heavy drops of sweat course down his sunburnt cheeks; and he sees that when they have surfeited themselves with drink and food, they sicken from the excess just as he, the labourer, does when he neglects the prudential rules of temperance and moderation; that when age creeps over them their hair whitens, and their limbs totter, just as is the case with him and his compeers; that when an epidemic rages and mows down the hard-working classes and those who live in penury, it spares not the palaces of the rich and great, but garners them in likewise into an untimely grave; and that, finally, should all things go well with them for many, many years, they cannot escape from the gaping, yawning tomb, though it be a pyramid which covers their dust, or a mausoleum which rises above their mouldering bones. It is, therefore, I say, that the humblest labourer feels within himself that he is a human being, equal with the highest; that he has hopes and wishes which carry him beyond the narrow space in which he dwells here; that he has a right to look forward to the time when he is to exchange his coarse attire for garments of light and glory, when he is to be the immediate servant of God instead of being dependent on, and subject to the arbitrary will of man.

This future equality of all the sons of Adam, however, is only possible on the assumption that there is a Power who can effect this change; for in human possibility it is not, and all the dreams of the philanthropist must, however well intended, end at length in sore disappointment. We may deplore the evil which meets us at every turn, we may weep for the tears of the innocent which we see flowing unrestrained; but we have no means of altering the lamentable state of things which meets our view. But when we look upward to the immeasurable sky, and behold millions of suns revolving around their common centre; when we reflect on the immense number of intelligent beings for whom all these vast worlds were created; when we contemplate on the immeasurable reach of that almighty Strength by which all this was called into being and is sustained without fatigue, without weariness, with watchfulness untiring, and with intelligence unflagging: we must come to the conviction that there is hope for the needy and consolation in store for the afflicted, of which nothing on earth can ultimately deprive them; since He, who is alike the God of the poor and the God of the great, is able to fulfil the desire of all the living, and heal the wounds of all those who suffer, and restore oppressed humanity to the full dignity of an immortal spirit.

It is owing to this that we so often find such expressions אני ה' or אני ה' אלהיכם "I am the Lord," or, "I am the Lord your God," as the reason assigned for the observance of any particular precept either of simple religion or morality; for instance: "And thou shalt not glean thy vineyard, and what droppeth in thy vineyard thou shalt not gather up; for the poor and the stranger thou shalt leave them; I am the Lord your God" (Lev. xix. 10), which Rashi explains, "I am the judge to demand recompense;" and so to verse 17, "Thou shalt not go about as a tale-bearer among thy people; thou shalt not stand idle by the blood of thy neighbour; I am the Lord," which is expounded, "Faithful to bestow reward, and faithful to bestow punishment." It is because God is ever living and ever present, consequently always ready and well informed of the affairs of men, that He is emphatically our God, and capable to supervise mankind to see whether or not they are faithful to their trust, and sedulous in fulfilling the various duties which He has assigned to them. In this respect now, namely, that there is but One Being to whom all are responsible, and all are compelled to look for the fulfilment of their wishes, we must consider all men upon one and the same level; wherefore it is also but just that all should have the same relative obligations towards each other. Station and wealth are merely accidental circumstances which in the present state of society must be assigned to the few for the benefit of the many; wherefore their possession does not absolve any one from the smallest requirement which is obligatory on others: and so likewise the humbleness of our position is no reason why we should permit ourselves trespasses and violations of the rights of our fellow-men; since neither the possession of worldly goods nor their absence can absolve us from a strict regard of the personal rights of our neighbours.

But it is not alone simple moral rules which the Scriptures contain, and which we are bound to observe; for there are other precepts which have reference more to the dependence which we have on God, as our immediate Sovereign, and which are not less necessary for our happiness, than the mere rights of humanity. I have already told you, that all duty depends on the revealed will of God; philanthropy, therefore, and charity in its most extended sense, are only obligatory on us because they are a part of the divine ordinances, which to enforce He announces himself as the Judge, who is sure to measure out a full recompense for our deeds, be this reward or punishment. But in order to impress us the more strongly with the acknowledgment of his sovereignty, and to render us thus the more energetically the friends of our species, He has assigned to us other duties, which in appearance only refer to our position toward the Lord alone, although they are secondarily calculated to govern our will, and to render us, therefore, more obedient in all other things. To this class of duties we may reckon the observance of the Sabbath and festivals, as also the resort to places of worship, wherein the name of God is especially invoked. Our text accordingly says, in the same strain, as of the moral precepts, to which we have already referred: "My Sabbaths shall ye observe, and my sanctuary shall ye reverence, I am the Lord;" which close of the verse we may freely expound as the others, "Ready to reward those who obey me in this, and to punish those who wilfully refuse obedience." It says, then, that as much as we look to God to reward and punish us according as we are merciful and just, or the contrary, so also will our observance of Sabbath-keeping, and propriety in public worship, or the neglect thereof, entitle us to God's mercy or his wrath. It would detain us too long to exhibit all the requirements which the observance of the festivals of the Lord demand; we can only deal with generalities, and I must therefore confine myself to them. We may, therefore, inquire what effect will the keeping holy of a particular day have upon us? Simply this, that whenever it recurs it will impress on our mind the well-attested fact, that it is a part of the law revealed to us by our Benefactor, He who gives us life and intellect, who moreover extends to us his helping hand to aid us in our distress, just as He acted towards our fathers, when He appeared as the Avenger of their wrongs, and broke asunder the bonds of their slavery, and bade them go forth to an everlasting freedom. It is this God also who demands of us to be kind to the poor, and to love each other, inasmuch as we have been servants to Pharaoh in Egypt; consequently, the observing of any festival will awaken us to reflect, that in addition to the mere act of resting which we do as a religious duty, we offer our homage to the Lord for the benefits we have received from Him, under so many and varied circumstances, and we tell at the same time, that we will do something, however little it may be, to deserve the continuance of his mercy; consequently, we shall be incited to make the rest from labour a happy day to all our dependents, to grant them a respite from toil, so that they too may have leisure to devote their thoughts, withdrawing them from the constant routine of exertion, to the reflection on Him who made us all, both servants and masters, after his own image, which means, making man but little less than angels, by imparting to him an intelligent soul, which is destined to live forever.

This view of the Sabbatic rest is not a mere fancy, an oratorical figure of speech; on the contrary, it is a literal transcript of various texts of the Law, which any one, who is even moderately familiar with it, will readily recognize. It is therefore quite proper to distinguish it as one of those precepts for which especially reward and punishment are indicated by the addition of the words "I am the Lord;" for, as respects our fellow-creatures, the brute even, it inculcates humanity the most elevated and universal, since all shall rest, and on God's day all shall cease from toiling, all shall be refreshed and recover new strength for the coming period of labour, and all shall thus have leisure to rise from the earth, and elevate themselves above its cares and disappointments, and enjoy a day of undisturbed serene repose; a fit emblem of the repose of everlasting life, when the labour of the child of sorrow shall be over, and no more shall be heard the groans of those heavily oppressed. And as regards our relation to the Creator, we testify, by our devoting to Him one-seventh part of our time, that we believe in his having made us; that we trust in the correctness of his word, which teaches us that outward nature is not a necessary pre-existing thing, but the effect of his potent will, which called all forth, and it was made, when He commanded that *it should*, and everything stood forth obedient to his nod. And there is need for us all so to acknowledge God in our heart and in our deeds; we all are apt to forget that we are accountable, we are all too eager to lay up treasures in this world, to labour for self-aggrandizement, for the advancement of ourselves and our immediate connexions; we fancy that success is in our hands, that we can mould circumstances to our purposes; we forget that we ourselves are but flowers of the moment, that are easily cut down broken and scattered to the four winds of heaven; and the longer we continue to toil, the more we become self-reliant, the less are we troubled by the reflection that our end is drawing on apace. If, however, we occasionally halt for a period; if on the weekly rest which we devote to God, we impress on our mind that it is not by our strength, but by his blessing that prosperity attends us as a handmaiden, ready at our bidding: we shall be humbled in his presence and think less of time than eternity, and be willing to listen to his commands, and take Him as our Counsellor in every period and phase of our existence.

So it is also with the other precept which our text contains, "And my sanctuary shall ye reverence," as it is likewise calculated to engender fear of God and love for man. The house where the name of the Most High is invoked, is not designed for those only who live at ease, but for all who feel themselves burdened with the weight and afflictions incident to the human state. The poor has indeed sore necessity for seeking the aid of his God, who is ever near to listen to his cry; the affluent, however, is not exempt from cares and troubles, and the brightest day seldom passes away without some little cloud, to obscure the brilliancy of our horizon; he too should therefore not be absent when the worshippers assemble to do honour to their glorious King, especially on the festivals and Sabbaths, when a universal repose dwells among the children of Israel. The sanctuary is to unite all the sons of man in one brotherhood, it is to encircle them with a universal bond of love and attachment towards their God and towards each other; one shout of praise should burst from all lips, one universal acclamation should attest the faith of all in the One who is the sole Lord and Saviour of mankind, and one feeling should animate all, to leave nothing undone to attest the sincerity of their faith and the truth of their attachment to their religion, which is the immediate gift of the Supreme, and which all our forefathers received as their portion when they exclaimed, "Whatever the Lord hath said will we do." Thus acting, we shall best testify that we believe in the Lord as the Rewarder and Avenger, and we shall thus earn his approbation, and prepare ourselves for that happiness which is the treasured portion of those who love Him and keep his commandments. Amen.

Nissan 29th.
May 1st. } 5611.

DISCOURSE III.

TRUE AND FALSE WORSHIP.*

Father of Israel! we call on Thee for thy blessing and thy aid, to be with us when we rise up to pursue our daily toil, and also then when we are engaged in thy service and in the study of thy law. For if we labour without thy blessing, we sow for nought; and if Thou sendest not the rain, the seed we plant will not shoot up from the ground; and if thy sun does not send down the light and heat with which he is

---

* Delivered on the second day of Pentecost, 5611, at the Synagogue Beth Israel, Philadelphia, by request of the Congregation.

endowed by Thee, the fruit will not ripen, and the corn will rot in the field. But also in spiritual things we are nothing without thy help. Vain and proud of our intellect, confiding in our experience, we would stumble in the plain path of duty, were we not enlightened by Thee—had we not thy wisdom to guide us safely. It was therefore thy will, O most holy God! to descend before the visible eye of thy children, to let them see thy glory, and to let them hear thy potent voice; and from the fire Thou spokest to their outward senses, that they might know thy law, to fear Thee and to love Thee, that they may live forever. And therefore, we entreat Thee, be not wanting to us at this day, and be graciously pleased to open our minds to receive the full impression of thy greatness and holiness, that we may be enabled to appreciate the commandments which we have received, that we may follow thy guidance, rejecting the inspirations of pride and self-conceit, which would counsel us to prefer worldly glory to thy favour, carnal pleasures to thy service, and self-aggrandizement to the love of our neighbour, as we are commanded in thy law. Yea, remove from our path the stumbling-stone of sin and temptation, and give us full understanding of our subjection to thy gracious Providence, in order that we may live as Israelites, as men in covenant with Thee, who, in obeying Thee, have obtained thy good-will, which is life everlasting, and the unending pleasures of spiritual delights, which are at thy right hand, stored up for the righteous, in whom Thou findest pleasure, which no eye has seen save thine alone, O God! our Redeemer and King. Amen.

Brethren!

One of our ancient prophets, one of those chosen by God to diffuse a knowledge of his being and will among men, thus spoke in the holy enthusiasm with which he was filled at the contemplation of sin around him:

הוי אמר לעץ הקיצה עורי לאבן דומם הוא יורה
הנה הוא תפוש זהב וכסף וכל רוח אין בקרבו : וה'
בהיכל קדשו הס מפניו כל הארץ : חבק' ב' ט' כ' :

"Wo to him who saith to the wood, Awake! Rouse up! to the inert stone. This should teach? Behold, it is set in gold and silver, and no spirit whatever is in it. But the Lord is in his holy temple; be silent before Him, all the earth." Haba. ii. 19, 20.

This is the festival of the promulgation of the law on Mount Sinai, when the Lord appeared in a manner never before or since witnessed, to instruct mankind in his will. This was an event which is most fitting to be celebrated whilst the earth stands—whilst the seasons follow each other in their ceaseless succession—whilst the sun shines as a light by day, and the moon and the stars rule the night; for by it we were lifted up from the ignorance of the nations, and were brought into connexion with the Creator, to serve Him alone, and to know no other god and saviour. Let us therefore dwell on the words of the prophet which have been quoted to you, in order to draw from them such lessons as are fitting to the occasion, since the festivals of the Lord are not seasons for mere rejoicing, but are all זכר ליציאת מצרים a memorial of our going out of Egypt, which means incentives to recall to our minds the benefits we have received, and the duty which rests on us to be grateful to our eternal Benefactor.

Habakkuk, in common with most of the prophets whose works have come down to us, preserved in the canon of the Bible, lived at a time when fearful sin had usurped the place of the worship of the Lord, which the law was given to institute. Israel had indeed departed from the way of righteousness, and their land was full of idols, and the number of Judah's gods was equal to that of its cities. The instruction of the sages learned in the history and legislation of their people was not sought; but the sinful multitude resorted to priests of falsehood and deceptive oracles to tell them what the future would bring forth. The temple at Jerusalem was not visited; but, instead of this, men rushed to the altars at Dan and Beth-El, wherefore the last was called by the prophets Beth-Aven, meaning no longer the house of God, as it was named by Jacob, when he dreamt of the angels who watched over his flinty pillow, but the house of iniquity, as it had become through the enormous transgressions of the chosen people. Therefore did God send fearless men, who only saw in their fellow-beings perishable creatures, whose anger they could well despise, and whose vengeance they could well defy, in the holy work for which they were designed, to lead back the erring children to the embrace of the Father who wished for their reconciliation. Hence we have the long list of prophets and teachers, who faltered not before the frown of despots, and halted not in the presence of a riotous multitude, though carnal weapons were lifted up against them, and they knew that by their perseverance their hours would be few on earth. They, however, taught boldly against the prevalent follies of their age. It mattered nothing in their estimation that it was the king who said to the wood, " Thou art my father," or that the high-priest spoke to the stone, "Thou hast borne me;" for their mission was from on High, and they regarded not the earth nor its allurements, in view of the great destiny which was theirs.

Therefore says Habakkuk, ." Wo to him who saith to the wood, Awake." Yes, so senseless had the people become in that generation, that they felled a tree in the forest, cut it into pieces, and fashioned a portion into the shape of a man, to stay with them in the house, whilst the other was perhaps used to bake the very bread they ate; and then they fell down on their knees before it, and addressed it in the words of prayer, in order to invoke the assistance of the idol, the fancied god, which had been made from a block of wood by the skill of the sculptor, and the decorations of gold and silver which it exhibited being merely the tinsel trappings of a cunning artisan, who had perhaps exhausted his genius in thus adorning the work of his hands, to render it a fit object of worship to himself and others. Now, behold, the idol is done; it is introduced into a gorgeous temple, with magnificent portico and elaborate ceiling; the light of day is mellowed into a dreamy twilight by a skilful arrangement of the windows; a refreshing coolness is spread around, even in the midst of noonday heat, by means of sparkling fountains gushing forth from a variety of fanciful forms, discharging the watery element into snow-white marble basins; heavenly music re-echoes along the dome from many high-sounding instruments and mellifluous organs; a cloud of sweet incense obscures the view, as it rolls along, opens and closes, wafted by the slightest puff of air which circulates through the vast space within the fane; numerous priests, with snowy robes, rude habiliments, or magnificent attire, are there to participate in the ceremonies of the day; and there stands the idol, dressed out with all the meretricious art which a diseased imagination can conceive, either in the shape of a beautiful youth, a grim warrior, a sage counsellor, a sweet maid, a ripe virgin, a shameless woman, a monster with many heads and arms, with head or feet of beasts—nay, even the figure of a brute or reptile; and all shout, "Rise and help us, for thou art our god." Or suppose that a long time they have been calling on their object of worship to come to their aid, and no heed is taken of their cries, no answer is given to their entreaties; in vain has flowed the blood of a hundred victims; to no purpose have been the gifts that were poured into the coffers of the deceivers: and a servant of the true God mocks them, and says, "Call with a louder voice, for he is a god; perhaps he is engaged in conversation; perhaps in a battle; perhaps he is on a journey; peradventure he sleepeth, and may wake up." What reply can they make, who so surrender their sound judgment to the inspirations of folly and self-deception? What matters it that the statue of their god is formed in the highest style of art?—that the temple itself is fashioned so as to challenge admiration from all beholders, and is destined to endure for ages? Does all this invest the wood with life and knowledge, and impart intellect and power to the inert stone?

You will think it strange that intelligent men ever could be thus misled to fall down in worship before deities thus fashioned; that enlightened states could legislate to institute different orders of priesthood, to attend to the large variety of idols which were set up all over the land; nay, that even mariners did not venture to sea without devoting a part of their vessel to the tutelary gods, as they conceived them, to which they paid adoration. You cannot understand how the mind could so far go astray, and lose itself in the labyrinth of folly; but so it is recorded in history that these things were, and so it is witnessed in distant lands that idols yet claim the homage of mankind, and that enormities are practised, at which humanity shudders, and which degrade man in ferocity and recklessness below the level of the brute. Most of you have no doubt heard of the practice of women burning themselves alive on the funeral piles of their deceased husbands, as though they thereby performed a religious duty; of crowds falling down to let the idol-wagon, with its enormous weight, pass over to crush them into shapeless masses, a willing and senseless sacrifice to brutal superstition; of men who devote themselves to murdering on the highway any unfortunate travellers who may fall into their hands, imagining that in this manner they bring an acceptable sacrifice to their abominable goddess, in whose mission they travel far and wide, to extinguish, by cunning, craft, or open violence, the sacred life of their fellow-beings. But it is not necessary to enumerate all the horrors of idolatry, as it is at the present time, or to exhibit the degrading effect it has on the soul; much less will it be requisite to go back to antiquity for illustrations which are met with on almost every page of history. All this only shows how weak man is without God—how utterly helpless he is, if the Almighty's wisdom and strength do not support him. Boast not, therefore, that you, my hearers, would not be so silly—that you could not have sunk so low, if, instead of being educated as Israelites, you had been instructed by Brahmins. Believe not in your own superior endowments; for, however our faith is congenial to our minds, however true it is that the doctrine of the unity of God has found its strongest supporters and defenders among the descendants of Jacob, do not imagine that we are not liable to fall away from the truth, if ever we are neglected in our early training, or that unhappy period should arise, as it almost was in the time of Menasseh and Amon, kings of Judah, that the law be nearly forgotten among us. For it was in those disastrous times, and previously thereto, during the reign of other wicked kings of Judah and Israel, that the prophets of God and the chosen teachers of Jeshurun were not permitted to speak in the name of the Lord; yes, we doomed to capital punishment those who were bold enough to reprove the backsliding of their sinning brothers, and a Zechariah and Isaiah thus perished, besides many others, but more especially in the reign of Ahab, in the fulfilment of their mission How ignobly did we then sink—how deeply were we fallen—when, like the uninstructed heathen, we resorted to our idols of wood and stone, which, when called upon, could not be awakened—which, when entreated, could not be roused up, to ask of them for advice and counsel, and when we came to the priests of deception to unravel for us the dark and unknown volume of the future. But do not for a moment imagine that there were not powerful means resorted to, to deceive the people, so that even the intelligent might occasionally be startled by the uncommon and strange coincidence which the event accomplished had to the cunningly devised prediction; for there have been at all times persons who flourished upon the degradation of their fellows, and who made the follies and vices of others subservient to their own advantage, or who, without any profit to themselves, rejoiced in becoming the corrupters of their race. Hence the means of deceiving were reduced to a perfect system, and you could scarcely frame a question to which the priests of darkness were not able to contrive some cunning, double-meaning reply. Now, observe, the morals of the age had become corrupt; the voice of instruction had been effectually silenced so far as the masses were concerned; a more showy worship was introduced, and this everywhere, than that exclusive, simple, awfully silent one at Jerusalem; every one that chose could be a priest, and the sons of Aaron were not the only ones who could claim the right to offer sacrifices, for here was a system in which all who chose might participate; add to which that answers about the future could be obtained, such as they were, at all times, by every one who had the means of satisfying the avarice or ambition of those who duped the simple, whether they were high or low: and you have some solution to the curious phenomenon that Israelites ever could have been idolaters. Perhaps some of you have even doubted the evidence of Scriptures about the universality of the defection.

Some may have even gone so far as to suppose that the prohibition against image-worship could not have existed among us till after the rebuilding of the temple, at the return of our remnant from Babylon, since when idolatry has never been practised *nationally* among us. But such an assumption would be against the evidence of history; and, however mortifying the confession must be, we cannot deny that Israelites have often lapsed into error regarding the nature of God and the worship of other divinities; and though these apostates from the truth cannot claim the benefit of conviction in favour of their adopted creeds, whether these be Nazarene, or Mahomedan, or absolute heathenism, they certainly have outwardly assumed the religion and manners of our opponents, and their children will assuredly be hostile to Israelites, and aliens to our faith; and if you examine into the families of every European and Asiatic nation, you will find among them the descendants of Jews, and these are not less devout and zealous in the service of the popular religions than those descended from their original professors, if any such can really be found, except among the people of Hindostan and the countries farther to the east thereof. And, though European nations have not that gross idolatry which prevailed in ancient Greece and the modern East, their belief is not less injurious to our peace and permanence than the worst system that ever was invented. Tell me not that to pray through a mediator is but a small offence; say not that to believe in the abrogation of the ceremonial law is a harmless error; imagine not that to permit us to mingle silently with the other families of man is not destruction to Israel.

No, Israelites, no! He is a traitor to your God who would permit himself to address any being save Him alone who is the Creator of all; who would believe in the asserted plurality of the Blessed One, like whose oneness—simple, uniform, uncompounded—nothing else exists. He is a renegade to truth who asserts that any change has taken place in the Almighty's holy law—that one jot or tittle has passed away from all that the Lord our God has taught us. And he is an enemy to Israel who would in the least weaken your attachment to your own nation, one and entire—a family of priests, as you are all, amongst whom no unaccepted stranger dare to mingle.

Still, brethren, we have known that such apostates have been; that some have left us who could not claim ignorance as their excuse; who could not even plead in their defence a pressure from without, and the weight of intolerable tyranny. Hence, if even our sufferings did not attest the fact, we should have ample reason not to doubt of the authenticity of Israel's shame; that almost universally they called on the wood to "Awake," and spoke to the stone, "Rouse up," at the period when the prophets were sent early and late to induce them to return from their evil path; but they would not, until the wrath was poured out, and they who would not receive correction when they possessed all that could embellish life, had to go forth, naked and famishing, into captivity, driven out of their lovely inheritance by the fire and sword of their enemies. Yet this signal chastisement was needed, to root out the evil from our hearts, and to implant therein an abiding love for our faith. Hard was the lesson, and dreadful the teachers that enforced it. Kindness and affectionate appeals would not move us. It therefore required the unbending will of arbitrary men, who could hear, without flinching, the groans of the dying on the field of battle, and who spurned the uplifted hands of the petitioning widow, who interceded on her knees for the life of her sole surviving offspring. And thus we wandered abroad, chased by day by the savage hosts of our invaders, and by night by the fear of our own hearts, which would not let us rest. Well, therefore, commences the prophet with the awful "Wo," "Wo to him who saith to the wood, Awake." Yes, wo in this life, wo in the next, to him who, living in the world which the Undying One has formed, still doubts of his providence and power, and addresses his prayer to the carved block, or calls for aid on the sculptured stone, or inquires of the things set in gold and silver for counsel and advice, or who entreats a god who cannot save, "who has no spirit whatever in him." And now that we are here, no longer in dread of our life because of the adversary, let no one be deceived, that he may swerve from the truth, either by permitting his children to go astray, either through uncircumcision, or by intermarriage with gentiles, or by an habitual disregard of the ceremonial laws, by all which a gradual amalgamation is necessarily brought about, or by direct apostacy, by which the union with Israel is at once severed, without danger of retribution; for the same God who denounced his anger against those who lived at ease and in plenty in their own land, defying the commandments which they had received, still lets us hear his "Wo" against all who, either themselves, or through those they might have restrained, but did not, call on any one in whom there is no spirit whatever, who is not the Creator, and has, therefore, no share or portion in the salvation of mankind.

It was not, understand, brethren, to teach a merely relative truth to mankind—by which I mean something which is less pernicious than another system, which is only in a less degree false and evil, but an absolute truth, or an idea which, if compared with whatever you will, is true, and only so as it is in every view you take of it—it was only to teach the absolute truth, that God revealed himself to our forefathers in all his inconceivable glory, on the first Pentecost after their redemption from slavery. He taught us then what we yet repeat to our children, to our brothers, to ourselves, that there is but one God, and there is no one else; in the words of the Decalogue, אנכי ה' אלהיך "I am the Lord thy God," not "we are," which might perchance imply a multitude of divine beings, though our reason would reject this doctrine upon the basis of our history, inasmuch as the same uniform Power has always been with us; but "I am," one, and only one, without a second to rule and save, just as there was but one to redeem us from thraldom, and just as there was but one at the creation of all things. Whatever else is offered to us as an object of worship, is a being in which there is no spirit whatever, be this the idol carved out by the hands of the cunning workman, or an ideality, the invention of yet more cunning deceivers;—they are all to be rejected, because their worship would militate against the reverence and homage due to the Lord of all, whom we have been taught to acknowledge as all-pervading—who is the living God, the Lord of the dead and of the quick, the Master of earth and of heaven, the Creator of the first, and the Preserver of the last. As such He appeared before us, and as such his majesty illuminated the summits of Sinai, and spoke to our senses audibly and distinctly, so that there was not a servant in the camp of Israel who did not feel convinced that there is not a god in heaven and on earth, who can do like the works and mighty deeds of our Father.

We were chosen as the messengers of this absolute truth, and for generations many millions have ever proclaimed it aloud before friend and foe, amidst prosperity and the deepest affliction. The unity of God has been our battle-cry; and, perishing under the torture of the Roman tyrant, or at the stake of a Spanish Inquisition, we exclaimed, "The Lord is one," and closed our eyes to the earth, its joys and its sufferings; and from the howling desert and the raging sea there ever ascends the same exclamation; and, go where you will, the heart of the Hebrew re-echoes the familiar sound, "There is none else." And is this nothing to accomplish? Was it not a result every way worthy of the Almighty's power, to establish thus for himself a nation of witnesses—an unbroken chain of teachers, which stretches onward, onward, till the mind aches to fix the end? Yea, it was a glorious spectacle, that assemblage at Horeb; it was beautiful to see more than twenty times hundred thousand of men, women, and children, listening eagerly to the same beatifying announcement of an imperishable faith; but more glorious still is the continuance of the same race of witnesses, of the same people of listeners, who even now rise up when the Decalogue is proclaimed among them, to receive again and again the joyful message which is announced to them in the name of the Universal Father. And earth and heaven speak of his might, and millions of suns recount his goodness, and an endless number of planets attest his mercy, and all space is filled with his being, and all revolve, exist, and live in Him; and still He watches over all with paternal care; the highest angel veils his face before his throne; none may abide the effulgence of his light; and still He hears the orphan's prayer, and marks the cry of the needy one; and He feeds the hungry, and provides raiment for the naked, and saves the oppressed from a hand too mighty for them.

This is our God, one, great, eternal, omnipotent, and all-pervading; yet He delights in the worship of his creatures, and He who gives us all is willing to accept our gifts; He who is everywhere condescends to dwell in a house which we have built of perishable materials; and He who knows all our thoughts is ready to listen to our entreaty, when we humble ourselves before Him in our distress, or thank Him in our prosperity. Human reason would not, could not have invented such a religion; but it is to Him alone we look as the Author of our faith, as He is the Author of our life. Therefore, says the prophet properly, after exhibiting the folly of idol-worship, "But the Lord is in his holy temple; be silent before Him, all the earth." Go where you will, over land or sea, in sunshine or darkness, there is God; no space is free from Him, and no imaginable state of existence can be without his supervision. Let, therefore, wickedness tremble: the Lord is in his temple; the whole world is his house; the highest height is not too high, the lowest depth is not too deep for his power, or removed from his government. Let discontent be hushed; for all is from Him, and He elevates the one and humbles the other; and who knows what is best for us, who can tell but that joy might have caused us to forget our Maker, and that it is affliction alone which brings us back to his embrace? Let pride and arrogance lower their look at viewing the universal power of the Lord, who is so great, yet so humble; who dwells amidst the host of adoring angels, and yet disdains not to regard the contrite and lowly. Let the virtuous hope on amidst difficulties; for they are watched over unceasingly with more than a mother's love, with a tenderness which knows of no abatement; and let all and each reflect that whatever takes place on earth is treasured up in the book of memorial, and that at the appointed time all will be brought to light, and the good and the evil will receive the recompense due to their deeds.—Yea, the Lord is in his holy temple; universal nature is his dwelling; not a spot but is full of his might; and, though he accepts our service, it is that we may be blessed through our own merit, not that He may be more exalted. Be silent, therefore, before Him, all the earth, and let the afflicted hope on in the salvation of their God, and always know that their Redeemer liveth, to whom be praises forever. Amen.

Sivan 5th. } 5611.
June 5th.

DISCOURSE IV.

THE OBJECT OF OUR REDEMPTION.*

BRETHREN!

Let us thank God that He has, in his mercy, enlightened our minds by his wisdom, and bestowed on us a law of reason, and revealed unto us the truth of his being the Author of all that exists. Simple as are the moral duties, little as you may deem the expression "I believe in one only God," the search for them has often perplexed the wisest of men, and to this day there are multitudes, to whom the religious obligations and faith of Israel are matters of profound astonishment and wonder. Besides this, it took a long time to discipline ourselves, before we imbibed the lesson so that it became a part of our nature, and it was the especial work of God, because He loved our fathers, that we were brought unto his service; therefore, it is but proper in us to say, we are thankful for this signal favour.

Long was the captivity which had chained us to the soil of Egypt; severe also was the toil which we had to endure under the task-masters of the Pharaohs: when in the royal palace was trained the man who was destined to end this captivity, and to rend asunder the bonds of this slavery. Driven away from this

---

* Delivered at the Synagogue Nefuzoth Yehudah, of New Orleans, on Sabbath Shemoth, Tebeth 25th, 5612.

home of elegance, refinement, ease, and pleasure, we at length behold him feeding the flock of a chief of a neighbouring nation, whose daughter he had espoused as a wife. His banishment was owing to an offence which he had committed against the laws, in his zeal for his oppressed brother-Israelites, and alone and by the world forsaken, he wandered far away into the desert of Arabia, to tend his charge, and to follow his humble pursuit, so different from what ambition had painted to his early imagination, when an inmate of the royal mansion. Eighty winters had already passed over his head: perhaps, his once black hair had been whitened in the lapse of years: and still he had before his mind the picture of his oppressed brothers, groaning and toiling under the excess of the rigour with which they were treated. Perhaps, hope had perished in his heart of ever seeing their condition improved, and the early promise of his ancestor Jacob, that God would think of them, no doubt appeared to him the mockery of hope, the accomplishment of which seemed more remote with every day that elapsed. But were our fathers forgotten? Did their groans escape the wakeful ears of Providence? Assuredly not: He who regards all our ways had so ordained it, that we should be strangers, and held to labour in a land not ours for four hundred years, in order to train us to become fit to stand on the earth as the witnesses of Almighty Power. Ay, you will, perhaps, say, "God could have effected this without our bodily suffering, without causing us to experience that feeling of despair, which must, doubtless, have often seized on our forefathers, when they laboured without reward, and toiled without benefitting themselves." But, admitting this, it does not gainsay that the trials which we had to endure, made us look up to Heaven for that protection which we in vain sought for on earth. But, independently of this consideration, we must not forget that the early followers of the truth were but the members of one family, which, in the lapse of more than two hundred years after the emigration of Abraham from Chaldea, amounted to only seventy persons. What barrier would such a handful of men have opposed to the evil influence of false opinions all around them? Was it not to be supposed that in a very short time one by one would have dropped off and mingled with the masses around them? Do we not see even at this day, that persons become tired of presenting the singular spectacle of being conforming Israelites, and adopting the customs, manners, and religion of the gentiles? Might not prosperity and ease have led us away, when so few in number, to regard as of no importance our separate national existence? No doubt but that this would have been the case to a great extent, at least, just as at present, when we see similar causes producing similar results. But now observe the ways of Providence:—Barely had the family of Jacob begun to multiply in the country assigned to them for their residence, than the antipathy of a difference of faith produced its natural result, a dislike of the majority for those who differed from them, precisely as it is witnessed daily in our own experience. Yet not alone was this dislike manifested in a mere unwillingness to acknowledge the Israelites as equals, though they had greatly enriched the land of their adoption, which had so pressingly invited their first settling on its soil as agriculturists and shepherds: but it soon degenerated into a desire of subjugating them to the service of the state, first to diminish their increase by excessive toil, and then to prevent their quitting the country, which they had already benefitted by their presence.

On the one side, therefore, we behold the Egyptians tyrannizing over our forefathers, abominating them as aliens, maltreating them as entirely depending on their will and pleasure: whilst on the other, it was also natural that those who thus suffered, should sigh for their freedom, which they could only hope to gain by the overthrow of their masters. A mingling of the races, where the subsisting relation was only as tyrant and slave, was, in the nature of things, impossible; and sooner or later, a collision must have taken place, wherein one or the other would have been exterminated, when either the rage of the oppressed would have crushed the oppressors, or the power of these, have exterminated the insurgent hordes. Both alternatives have occurred in the history of the world, and would in our case have resulted in an obliteration of our entire people from the history of mankind, or presented us in our first rise as merciless murderers, and a horde of ruthless barbarians. In either case our residence in Egypt would have been without its influence on human events, so far, at least, as the progress of mind and civilization is concerned; and this would have been the result even if we had been victorious, until such time as the savage and rude natures, who had struck for freedom, had been reduced to a more gentle and tractable state. This might have endured for ages, as we have proofs that it has required these in other nations to effect the least good result; and then it is doubtful what form the new civilization would have assumed. But it is evident that the compulsory residence in Egypt of a family of men like ours is, highly intellectual and susceptible of the greatest improvement, could not lead to such deplorable results, without injuring in a material point the progress of human society. If the intention of Providence was to isolate us, it was not to render us barbarians; if it was designed that we should not be mingled up with other nations, it was not to arm us against all the world besides. How then was the liberation of Israel to be effected? Precisely as it is recorded, by the evident interference of Omnipotence, at the time when they had become sufficiently numerous to stand alone in the rank of nations, capable of maintaining an independence in government and opinions, against the assaults of all mankind.

Some of you may, perhaps, think that it is assuming too much to suppose that the course of events portrays to us the ways of Providence; but, on the other hand, let me ask you, "Wherein will you discover design and wisdom, if it be not in the succession of events which occur around us? Do you believe there is anything fortuitous? any occurrence which stands forth before us without its being within the supervision of the Most High?" Men are, indeed, free agents, empowered to work out in a minor degree the thoughts which arise within their hearts. Nevertheless, the whole course of recorded events proves this fact, that everything, notwithstanding this, tends towards the general good of God's creatures, or, in other words, that there is no unmitigated evil. Let, then, the wicked purpose and encompass in their mind the greatest injury to society, they will be debarred at once by the limits in which they are permitted to move, and which are a check on all events, from effecting their ends; and beyond the power of endurance of others they will not be permitted to work out their fell design. We are, therefore, empowered to assume, even if we had no revelation to guide us, that the residence of the Israelites in Egypt was not a useless period in their history, and that the sorrows which they had to encounter were not without their corresponding good results. We will, then, at once assert, that their residence in that country was designed to withdraw them for awhile from the close intimacy which had sprung up between them and the inhabitants of Palestine, whose corruption and immorality would have operated highly detrimental to their own prosperity; and the servitude they had to endure was in the same manner calculated to prevent their mingling with the refined but voluptuous and indolent denizens of the land of the Nile, and sinking, like them, into idolatry and moral inertness. The Psalmist, therefore, justly enumerates this fact amidst the objects of mercy for which he is grateful to the Lord; as we read: "And Israel came to Egypt, and Jacob sojourned in the land of Ham. And God multiplied his people greatly, and made it stronger than its enemies. He turned their heart to hate his people, to deal treacherously against his servants." (Ps. cv. 23–25.) And all this was done, we may assert farther, to impress on the conviction of this people, on the mind of these servants of God, the full knowledge of whose people and whose servants they were. They saw around them the prosperity of their masters, and they beheld them at the same time worshipping in the manner their own diseased fancy had taught them. Every virtue, every vice, every power of nature was deified and represented under some typical form, some monstrous figure of man, of bird, or of beast; the very cattle of the field were held sacred and worshipped, or, at least, regarded as the emblem of some superior power, even on the assumption that idolatry represented deeper and higher ideas among those initiated in its mysteries, than it did among the vulgar crowd. And yet when the time came for the contest between the truth and the falsehood, between the living God and the base inventions of darkness, it was made manifest that the Lord is the only God in heaven and on earth, and that there is none else; his will had to be obeyed, and, though unwillingly, Pharaoh had to consent to let Israel go free, in obedience to the wonders and miracles wrought in his land, through the means of the messenger of Heaven.

But I anticipate what I was going to advance when referring to our history. Moses had come to the desert in pursuit of his humble calling, when his attention was arrested by what could not fail of striking with awe the spirit of the most courageous,—a bush was flaming in fire, yet not diminished of its substance, notwithstanding the fierce combustion to which it was subjected; and whilst about preparing to investigate this phenomenon, so much in accordance with the history of his people, then and since, he for the first time obtained an insight into those great truths for which he had hitherto sighed in vain. The voice of

Almighty Power fills his ears with audible sounds, like which nothing human can be imagined; it is not merely hearing, but a full conviction that it is so, and not otherwise, which comes over him, and his foot is arrested on the sacred soil where the mighty Presence is revealed, and he feels strengthened and endowed with a new vigour to undertake the noblest mission which ever fell to the lot of man, to be the harbinger of freedom and the herald of truth to the oppressed and unenlightened, and the light and guide to his fellow-creatures for all ages which are to be on earth. And so spoke the God of our fathers, "I am the God of thy father, the God of Abraham, the God of Isaac, the God of Jacob," and all uncertainty which the inventions of Egypt's priests may have produced in his soul at once fled, and he recognized that all their dreams were vanity, and that there exists none to share the power of the One whom Abraham, Isaac, and Jacob had worshipped. The traditions of his fathers rushed through his soul; the false teachings of the priests of Egypt and Midian, if ever they had the least influence on his spirit, vanished forever, and he recognized in its full extent the existence of one sole God and Ruler, and that no other being can be imagined as sharing his power and glory. But the very reminding that this God was the one worshipped by the patriarchs must have excited in him the deepest regret at the long servitude of their children, seeing that they were to all appearances forsaken and left to the mercy of their oppressors. He may have thought that, if the covenant with Abraham was yet remembered, why did his children languish and groan under intolerable wrongs? But if Moses so reflected, his thoughts were not long permitted to flow in that channel, as he was notified that full cognizance had been taken of the sufferings of the Israelites, and that the fulfilment of the promises made to the patriarchs should be no longer delayed. The manner of effecting this was next made known to him; since he himself was appointed the messenger of the Divine Will to Pharaoh to demand the liberation of Israel. To this, however, Moses objected, alleging his unworthiness for the great work assigned to him. Be it that Moses actually uttered the words which we find recorded, or that he merely thought so, and revolved in his mind the difficulties of the task before him, it is all the same; and well did it become him not to rush upon the glorious mission with hot and eager haste, as many of inferior powers would assuredly have done; and not until he felt convinced that he could not fail, would he consent to make the attempt, even in obedience to a divine command.

But this assurance was not long withheld; for he was told,

כי אהיה עמך וזה לך האות כי אנכי שלחתיך בהוציאך את העם ממצרים תעבדון את האלהים על ההר הזה : שמות ג' י"ב'

"For I will be with thee; and this shall be unto thee the proof that I have sent thee, when thou hast brought forth the people out of Egypt,—you shall serve God on this mountain." Exod. iii. 12.

This means, that not by human power, not by the clash of weapons, not by the shock of contending hosts, should the accomplishment of the prediction be brought about, but by a chain of resistless events, which would leave the tyrant no other means of escape than an entire yielding to the demand which Moses was to make in the name of God. The prophet was, therefore, thus answered, when he asked, "Who am I, that I should go to Pharaoh?" Indeed, in his own person he had little power; he was but a lone shepherd of the desert, banished from his native land, unknown to his fellow-Israelites, whom he was to redeem from bondage, without wealth or influence anywhere, in danger of his life, so far as human probability was concerned, in case he should be denounced to the civil authorities, if he ventured to return unpardoned from his banishment. Consequently the assurance came with a double force when the Lord told him, "Go, because I will be with thee:" nothing shall be too difficult to be overcome, and no danger too great to be withstood, since the Most High himself would protect and prosper his messenger; hatred should be converted into respect, unwillingness into submission, before him who was to come shielded by the protection of the Supreme, until that time when the accomplishment should have crowned the attempt with complete success. And more yet, a new assurance was given, one even greater than the mere freeing the people from earthly bondage, that, when they should have left the land of their servitude, they should also be freed from the vices and superstitions of the priests who there taught their errors; and the Israelites, thus released from thraldom to the king, should learn a new and free worship, a religion of truth and mercy, and serve in a pure faith the God of reason and truth at the mountain where Moses then first heard his Maker's voice. And the very impotence of the idols of Egypt and their worshippers was to be exhibited clearly and conclusively as a preparatory step to this double enfranchisement; goodness and justice were to be conjoint in effecting the will of the Most High: so that the obduracy of the king was to be coerced in consenting to the liberation of his serfs, and these were to see that an Almighty Hand had guided them forth to freedom and light.

We have thus before us this conviction, that the stay of the Israelites in Egypt was not to punish them for any wrong done by them individually or collectively, but to teach them nationally the power and goodness of God. A people was needed on earth to guard the truth of God's being the sole Author of all, a truth which each successive generation had rejected as too little in accordance with the pursuit of pleasure and selfishness. It was, therefore that, at the very time the Lord promised to Abraham a numerous progeny, He also foretold him the sufferings which they should have to endure. Our ancestor did not complain, though a dark, deep melancholy overcame him, assured that all would result for the best of the world. He did not, perhaps, understand how such great sufferings could well lead to so great an end; still he did not lose his confidence in Him who had so long guarded him in his own wanderings. Nor was his trust misplaced. During all the servitude of the Israelites, though so many perished, the great aim constantly became more and more developed; a nation was reared, hardy, strong, and laborious, so unlike all others raised under a southern sun; and they must have felt at the same time that they would owe a debt of everlasting gratitude to whomsoever would or could release their limbs from the galling chains with which they were loaded. Had it been a man, they perhaps might have deified him, as was the foolish practice of the age in which they lived: what else then could they do, but be drawn to the service of that invisible Being, who in his might passed through the land at the dark midnight hour, and at whose nod sank unto death the first-born of every house? Then arose wailing and weeping from the hearts of the obdurate who refused to recognize the power of the Supreme, and the slaves were sent forth to freedom, and their hands were not stained with blood, and their garments reeked not with the gore of their slain adversaries; but they rejoiced in the victory which Justice had achieved, and they praised the Power which had triumphed without effort over the weak designs of impotent men.

No wonder, then, that our forefathers were ready to follow their God into the trackless desert, that they promised to obey and to do whatever might be taught them from on High. And though the ancient force of habit occasionally overcame their newly-begotten faith, though they at times sighed for the fleshpots of Egypt: they again returned to their allegiance when they were reminded that the same Justice which had humbled their oppressors, was also ready to chastise them for their forgetfulness of duty. And never has the faith which our fathers received at their first liberation been entirely forgotten; thousand and thousand times have we rebelled; again and again have we offended; frequently did our enemies predict, at least they pretended to hope, that our national extinction was nigh and impending: still at each period the God of Abraham came to our aid, and saved us from the devouring sword of our adversaries, or, when prosperity had made us forgetful of our allegiance, He stretched forth the rod of his vengeance, and called us back to his service by the afflictions which robbed us of our ease and greatness.—And, brothers, who is this God whom we were taught to worship? Do you know how He is called? Can you tell me the name by which He bade Moses call Him when He announced himself as our national God, as the worshipped of our fathers? Did He call himself mutable? mortal? insufficient? short of days? weak in power? O no,—it is as אהיה אשר אהיה, "I will be, the One who ever will be," that He revealed himself to Moses, and as He commands us to acknowledge Him in all our generations, so long as there is one son of Israel to stand before Him on the earth which He has created. And what does this name, "I will be," signify? Simply that He is alone in his power and eternity; He is the sole one who can say of himself that He will exist forever, to the infinitude of time, which even imagination in vain tries to limit or measure; who was before all creation, who is whilst all created things exist, and who will nevertheless continue, though all of which we have a conception shall have faded again into nothingness, and this vast structure of the universe shall have sunk again into the Being whence it has sprung.

Yes, the mind wanders almost into madness to reach even in approximation the greatness and eternity of our God. How utterly impossible is it, then, to define what He is! He declared himself as "I will be;" and as such let us adore Him, and bring to his service our whole heart and soul; let us surrender ourselves entirely to his holy keeping, in the full assurance that whatever betides us is, at last, for our own happiness. But let us also beware how we swerve from our God, and forget that line of duty which our forefathers pledged themselves and their children to pursue. For, behold, it is not an arbitrary mandate which we regard as our religion; it is the conviction that our fathers received the true knowledge of the nature of the Godhead, which we manifest in our obedience; and who will dare to say that the knowledge which we then obtained is not applicable at this day to the Almighty, who is, from his very being, unchanging? What could have come into existence since then to limit his power or to circumscribe his mercy? Who of his creatures has since then arisen to teach Him wisdom, or to aid Him in the accomplishment of his will? And who are we—we who are here this day? Ay, recipients of the same bounty which our fathers obtained. And what were they called upon to do? Only to observe the precepts which they had received, as a token that they believed in the Being who had so signally loved and blessed them and their predecessors. And was there ever a time when there was a break in this great chain of mercies and truths? when the Lord was no longer almighty, or we not dependent on his goodness? Where, then, is the permission for us to relax in our task, whilst He changes not in his power and mercy? Why shall we neglect his commandments, which are the sign that we are devoted to the only true God—to the sole Creator—the only Ruler and Protector of the universe?

Ay, you may say, He needs not our services to make Him happy. But it is not for his sake, but for ours, that we are to be faithful; we were chosen to be his witnesses, to testify by our presence that we believe in no other god than Him who created all things; and, therefore, in order to preserve us from mixing with those who walk not in the light of the Lord, are we commanded to seal our children with the sign of the covenant, that we and they may know that we are consecrated to his service; therefore do we keep the seventh day Sabbath, in order to testify that we believe in the creation of the world; therefore do we eat the unleavened bread to show that we have full faith in the truth of the revelation which was communicated to us at the time we went forth from Egypt; therefore do we write a copy of the law, that it may be a testimony against us whether we indeed observe the ordinances which have been taught us, as the emanation of the will of our Father, who is in heaven. But not for our own sake alone do we exist; but that we may always be as a light to the nations, so that at length all may reach that haven of divine truth, which will at one time embrace all the sons of man. In the meanwhile, let us be faithful guardians of the light; let us watch the sacred flame, in happy or in evil times; let us not be fainthearted, when it appears nigh its extinction; but let us, in the deepest time of distress, when the sinning of our nation is the darkest and the loudest crying for vengeance, not lose the courage which always animated us, and let us hope on forever in the ultimate accomplishment of all the good which the Lord has predicted for Israel. For, if the darkness of Egypt was changed into light, and history testifies that it was, the darkness which now lies heavily on us will also vanish. And the sun of righteousness will arise, and dispel the gloom which weighs down the spirit of those who grieve for the backsliding of Israel, and joy will illuminate again the heart of those who mourn for Zion. Let the wicked be ever so numerous; let ever so many throw off the yoke which we and our fathers promised to wear in the service of God; let the number of the faithful be reduced to the smallest fraction: there is still a life in the root of Israel which will survive all perils, and spring forth again to the light of day, at the time of the awakening, when the spirit of truth will walk abroad over the renovated earth; when a bright glory will encircle those who have waited faithfully the coming of the Lord to rule over all the sons of Adam; at that day, when all mankind will cast away their idols and vain imaginations, when all will call on the Most High with one voice; at that happy hour, when all will declare their belief in one God, and worship the Lord, who is one and alone, in the sincerity of faith. Amen.

Tebeth 22d.
Jan'y 14th. } 5612.

DISCOURSE V.

THE FALSE PROPHETS.*

ISRAELITES AND FRIENDS!

If we needed any confirmation of the truth of the Bible, it could be obtained from the simple fact that it contains passages which seem evidently to foreshadow all possible phases of our history, even to the present day; and the very state of confusion in which we find ourselves at this period, the agitation which now pervades the public mind, and which I expect you have this day come to hear me discuss, is according to my view fully indicated in Scripture. Let me remark beforehand, that I have hardly any hope of effecting any good by what I am going to lay before you to-day; for where the passions have become so much excited, where opinions, founded in reason or otherwise, are maintained in so determined a manner, it is not to be expected that a contradiction of them will be received with any good-will or favour. And hence I have no right to anticipate to meet with more indulgence than others would under similar circumstances. Moreover, people will accuse me of being personal, because they may assert that I speak of individuals well known to them, although I mention not their names. But in this I would be judged wrongly. If a preacher speaks of any infraction of the divine law, in great or small things, some one or the other will

---

* Substance of an address delivered in the Synagogue B'nai Israel of Cincinnati, on Sabbath, April 28th, 5615.

think that he hurls his denunciation mainly at him, although the subject be presented in general terms; and in the same manner is it with the topic embraced in my present address: I shall speak, indeed, of men and things, and if the number to be affected are but few as yet, it would, nevertheless, be unfair to suppose me guilty of personalities, or as meaning some particular one solely, since, unfortunately, the rebuke will fit a class, not an individual; the wrong alone must be condemned, and this without regarding what may be said or thought of the denunciation, or whom it may reach; and evil must not be hidden for fear that some person might think the admonition specially levelled at himself. If for such weak reasoning crime should have to go unrebuked, if every public teacher should be thus restrained by a vain dread of offending: no instruction could ever be conveyed from the pulpit; for every public address could then be chargeable as obnoxious to personalities for the reason advanced, that no offence against the Law of God could be touched on without some one imagining that his peculiar case had called forth the condemnation which has reached the ear of the people.

With this premised, let us turn to the twenty-third chapter of Jeremiah (23–27), where we shall find a passage perfectly applicable to the present state of Israel.*

"Am I a God for those near at hand, saith the Lord, and not a God for those who are afar off? If a man should hide himself in secret places, should I not then see him? saith the Lord. Do I not

---

* The translation only is here given; the Hebrew which was recited in the address is omitted, as not adding anything material to the subject, except in the speaking.

fill the heavens and the earth? saith the Lord. I have heard what the prophets have said, that prophesy falsely in my name, saying, I have dreamt, I have dreamt. How long shall it be in the heart of the prophets that prophesy falsehood, yea, the prophets of the deceit of their heart,—how long do they think to cause my people to forget my name by their dreams which they relate, every man to his neighbour, as their fathers forgot my name for the sake of Ba'al?"

We have indeed fallen on evil times when men put their dreams in the place of the revelation of God, and endeavour to subvert the customs of our forefathers for idle fancies. It is fearful to contemplate the vast amount of false teaching which is brought forward to mislead the people; and it is agonizing to reflect that the flocks have to watch the shepherds, and those who should be led, their leaders. In ancient times it was not so; for then we could securely follow the guidance of our teachers; we had only to ask them for advice, and we were safe; because we knew that they would only show and instruct us what is right. "The scholars of the wise brought truly much peace in the world;" and their words were full of the divine intelligence by which truth and righteousness were scattered abroad. But many of their modern successors have wofully failed to tread in their footsteps, but have substituted their own fancies and inventions in lieu of the pure doctrines of our religion. And still they tell us that there is peace, that there is union in the camp of Israel. But I tell you that there is strife, that there is disunion. Opinions have been made to clash against opinions, and diverging methods of explaining Scripture have been invented, and parties are ranged in hostile array against each other: and this you would call PEACE?

Yes, in words we have enough of peace; but in reality we have war within our once peaceful camp, when authority decided all matters of contest, and people yielded to the decision of their sages. Now, however, we have the fancies of wild theorists in the place of religion, and instead of mature wisdom we have DREAMS, and teachers of the kind in question grope in darkness, and each one gives us as truth what his imagination has invented, and he comes saying, חלמתי חלמתי "I have dreamt! I have dreamt!" And these should guide us? such as these should teach us what they think the word of God *should* be according to their prejudiced views?

O! there is a dark cloud resting on the future of Israel, an evil-foreboding mist envelops the course of our history, while no human eye can penetrate the obscurity which now excites our fears and apprehensions. And yet we are told that it is all well, that we may safely abandon the welfare of our cause to the new leaders who have come among us: whereas they prophesy, when God has not sent them, and they speak without a warrant from on High. But they mislead the people, inasmuch as, instead of teaching them to look to the law of God for instruction, to let divine wisdom guide them on the path of life, they hold up HUMAN REASON as a standard by which to measure Israel's faith and duties, and they flatter human vanity, in making our ideas, our conceptions, the arbiters of opinions and duties which confessedly have not, and could not have had their origin in mere human understanding. One evil resulting from this perversion is, that those who tell you to beware of your own judgment are not listened to with any degree of patience, they being viewed as behind the age, in not yielding obedience to the idol of the hour. Now this is the danger of which I have just been speaking, the dark portentous cloud which hangs over our future; for our enemies are from ourselves, —our destroyers, those who should help to build us up. Were a Catholic pontiff, a Protestant missionary, a Mahomedan Mufti, or the Grand Lama to come among us, each one to offer us his system for acceptance, it would not affect us greatly. We could laugh to scorn the pontiff who would pretend to his plenary power in matters of religion and church-government,—we would not believe him; the Protestant missionary who would offer us his divinity with power to mediate between us and our Almighty God, would be turned away with scorn and contempt, as our reason would at once revolt against his creed; we would reject triumphantly the invitation of the Mufti, who would bid us say, "There is one God, and Mahomed is his prophet," because we could on no condition attach any faith to one whom the Creator has not sent in his name; and surely not one of us would ever listen to the assumption of the Lama, that in him there is constantly a renewal of the divinity, as he represents himself to be. No, no; such as all these can work no permanent danger to Israel; none of these can seriously injure us. But if one of our own teachers rises up and tells us that in our own conscience, in our reason, we can meet with that guide which can lead us, without any fail or hindrance, on the toilsome journey of life: O then we listen with complacency; that pleases our fancy, that agrees so well with the inspiration of our indwelling pride, that administers so aptly to the wickedness of our stubborn heart, and we are gradually led away from the strict path of obedience to the absolute commands of God, and we install OUR WISDOM in the place where the PRECEPTS OF THE LORD should alone bear the government. Foreign gods we can resist; false prophets of other nations we may safely defy; they cannot injure us, for we never can adopt them as the controllers of our will. But far different is it with the idol that dwells within us; the inclination to evil which lies in wait for us in our own hearts, which is sure to overpower us when we lose sight of our accountability, and fancy that we can travel securely without the guidance of God, or that we can measure the justice of his enactments by the standard which our comprehension of things may set up as the proper measure of truth and right. Therefore we may apply to our teachers, who would so instruct us, the denunciation, "who think to cause my people to forget my name by their dreams, as their fathers forgot my name for the sake of Ba'al!" The heathen-idols were adopted by the Israelites that they might dispense with the strict obligation which God's religion imposed on them: in this they were encouraged by their false prophets, who invented dreams to impose, by a pretended revelation, on the masses. And if any, by encouraging us to follow our reason, produce the same effect on the public mind, to unsettle the attachment of Israel toward the law, and let each become the judge of what he chooses to do, without regard to authority: what is it but to cause us to commit the same iniquity for which Ba'al was the pretext among our ancestors? Are not such teachers in very truth "the prophets of the deceit of their hearts?"

But they will appeal to us, and say, "We are honest in our teaching, we only speak in consonance with the sincere dictates of our conscience, with what we conceive proved as the best and purest system of our religion." We will give them the benefit of this excuse in full. But if they be so honest, they need not be offended at our misapprehending their intentions; for there is One above who will be able to judge them rightly, if they suffer wrong at our hands; "for He, who will see a man though hidden in secret places," will not let them suffer any permanent injury from the injustice of erring and partial men. But, as human beings, we must decide the case according to the facts before us; and with these I am compelled to say, that under their teaching a degree of laxity of observance has been produced which was not known before these men arose among us. Sinning has always characterized the children of mortality; but the present agitation appears to be a systematic effort to render the defection permanent and incurable, and to install quite another measure of righteousness for Israel than the plain word of God, as we have been interpreting it to this very time. And in this the leaders of whom I speak have acted very unjustly. They have spoken in general terms, that a change was necessary; and when we called on them through public speech, or public writing, to define the limits of their intended progress, we obtained abuse instead of a calm reply. Instead of fairly laying down the principles on which the modifications of our religion should be made, by which all might have been enabled to judge of the legality and admissibility of the changes, we were received with scornful laughter, with ridicule and abuse; we, the orthodox, to use a familiar term, were denounced as ignorant, as behind the age, as incapable to understand the subject. But, my friends, however it may suit the lovers of the new order of things to denounce those who act with us, it is not true that we are all so ignorant, so unenlightened as our opponents pretend to think us. The light of science and discovery has risen for us also, and we have not been behind them, as a class, in the field of modern research and study. What they have learned, that we also have learned; and hence we yield not to them in any element necessary to comprehend justly the matter at issue. They know this; and they therefore ought to have developed their plan, and at once unfolded their principles of action. But silence on this point suited them better, and ridicule and denunciation were resorted to in place of sound argument. Yet grant for argument's sake that we were all so ignorant as has been represented: what would this be to the question? Cannot a scholar correct his teacher? cannot a child fittingly at times reprove his father? Yes, the Bible teaches, "Out of the mouth of babes and sucklings hast Thou founded strength;" those who are barely endowed with speech can teach us wisdom, can point out to us the glories of the kingdom of Heaven: why then should not the less learned, admitting they be inferior, be able to give advice to those who claim to know more than they? Did not a great doctor of our Mishnaic period relate, "Much have I learned from my teachers, more yet from my companions, but most of all from my scholars?" This indeed is the nature of wisdom, that one, no matter how much beneath another he may be, can at times point out to him wherein he has failed, wherein he can improve his knowledge or conduct, without thereby lowering his standing or dignity. If our modern reformers were therefore honest in their endeavour to improve the people, they would not always, boasting of their superior learning, scorn those they deem beneath them in this respect; but they would with proper deference reply to the questions which are fairly put to them, condescend to make use of some arguments, and not silence all debate by abuse and arrogance. This is not the way to enlighten the people; this is not the path of true wisdom; and bold denial is not the best method to convince the world of the falsehood or absurdity of long-cherished opinions.

The object, however, of such a proceeding is evident enough: they wanted merely to cast suspicion on the whole ancient order of things, in order to be permitted to make such revolutionary changes as their own diseased fancy might dictate, and to render Jews of the present day as different from ancient Israel as possible. How far they have succeeded, let the present confusion prevailing among us testify. Opinions clash against opinions, and we are threatened with being split up in sects; whereas formerly we were uniform in our practice, if we omit a small portion of men who are known, by a peculiar name, as a secession party. These modern men, therefore, have seized on the disorders prevailing frequently in our religious meetings and synagogues, and pointed them out as evidences that there was something radically wrong in our system. They said, that this want of decency proves that we must have reform in order to produce due decorum in the house of God. [*Here the speaker paused, because at that very moment there was much confusion, owing to several entering the synagogue, and causing some interruption in procuring seats; resuming then he said:*] The very disorder which has just taken place may perhaps be seized on to prove that a change is requisite in our mode of worship; that we must go out of our limits to find a model to imitate, in order to purify the Jewish synagogue, and that nothing short of customs foreign to the observances we have hitherto followed can save our structure from ruin. But it is not true that orthodoxy is chargeable with want of decorum in our places of worship. Our teachers require of us that we are not to converse during the prayers, nor during the reading of the law; that we are to behave in the synagogue at all times as though we stood in the immediate presence of our heavenly King; that when we come to pray we should direct our heart on High, and feel within our inmost soul what our mouth utters. Do you want any better rules for devotion? There can be none; ascribe, then, the confusion which prevails at times among you, not to orthodoxy, but to the want of attention so many pay to religion, to the tendency of the times to disregard the obligations of duty. The remedy then is not REFORM, as the word is usually used, but a RECURRENCE to ancient principles, to do what the teachers of Israel, the men of faith and piety, have laid down for our guidance.

The people ought to be told what is needed, what is required of them, and the heads of congregations should enforce the rules which Jewish worship demands, and all would be well,—confusion would be banished, the running in and out, which is so unseemly, would not shock those who come to offer up their devotion, and Jewish meetings would become the exemplars of assemblies for the adoration of Him who searches the heart. But what do our moderns aim to accomplish? Nothing less than to make you believe that disorder is inseparable from ancient Jewish manners; and that nothing can be done to save us from destruction, but change and revolution. Hence everything is too much, or not adapted to the times, unfitted to the present state of the world. And no doubt that they argue thus in their heart: "What! am I to spend two hours or three at the synagogue every Sabbath morning? am I to recite the prayers which my grandfathers used? am I to listen to a whole weekly section of the law as has been done so long? and all this in our present enlightened age? Impossible; it is more than can be expected of me!" And now let us look at the remedy; they will change the whole, so as to bring the attendance of the synagogue within the *convenience* of all, and they will therefore proceed after this fashion: we shall have a couple of pages of prayers, then have read one chapter of the Pentateuch, followed perhaps by a few select verses from the prophets; next we shall have a voluntary played on the organ, the new element of religion which is to be introduced, then a hymn sung by a trained choir; after which we shall listen to a sermon from a preacher who deifies human reason, and then we shall go home, after having another hymn and a closing voluntary on the organ.—[*Observing some token of merriment, the speaker paused and resumed:*] This is no subject for laughter, but one for weeping; yes, from the bitterness of my heart do I speak at the contemplation of such a profaning of our sacred worship. What! are we to have, instead of prayer, the strains of a hired choir, who sing a few words without feeling what they utter for our amusement? are we to have the opportunity to criticize the performance of the soprano, contralto, tenore and basso, with the usual manner of musical judges, and to accord the superiority to mere extraneous aiders in what is of right the business of all, to sing the praises of the Most High? Tell me, how can such psalmody improve the heart and purify the sentiment? how can preaching such as I have exhibited to you tend to lead the sinner back to God, and to arrest the man of iniquity in the course of crime?

No, not such a worship do we need; we want something more Jewish to satisfy the requirement of Israelites, at least if they would pray in earnestness and sincerity to their Creator. In the mode which our reformers wish to introduce, it must be evident that all which they design is to please those who come to the synagogue. They fancy that people do not attend now, because the forms are not attractive enough; the style of reading is too simple, or the prayers themselves are too long, or the language of our fathers does not suit the modern taste, nor can the method of enforcing obedience to the ceremonial practices of Judaism, in a sermon delivered by its pious teachers, correspond with the ideas of those who have ceased to hold the acts of religion in reverence. This would all be very well if the whole idea of public worship, prayers, reading, and preaching were merely predicated on pleasing the people, or if these would be doing all that is needed in coming only to be amused and entertained. Is it necessary to prove that all this is fallacious? I think not; for all worship would be self-glorification, not intended to humble ourselves before the Supreme Power, not calculated to bring comfort and consolation to an agonized spirit, and to recall us to better and holier feelings, to which perchance we have become strangers. We must not forget that the chief object of public worship is to pray in unison with our fellow-Israelites, so that one may incite the other to submission to the decrees of God, while all impress on themselves the conviction, in asking Him for all they need, that from the Lord alone can they obtain aid in their need, enlargement in their distress. If, then, I feel truly my dependence, if I have within me the consciousness of God's greatness and wisdom, and of my own dependence and littleness: I shall not find the time hang heavily on my hands which I spend in his immediate presence; two hours, or three on usual Sabbaths, or a longer space on the high festivals, will then seem a pleasant sojourn in the courts of the Lord, and I shall require no other incentive to pray and sing praises, than the consciousness that by words alone I can express the devotional sentiments of my heart. It has been said that it is best preaching to a religious community; since when one is alive to his duties, and is anxious to fulfil them, every reproof will be listened to with due respect, though the transgression be ever so small; as the pious is desirous to be kept in the path of righteousness by his own watchfulness and that of others. The same may be said with regard to prayer and the reading of the Scripture: a person must be in the proper frame of mind, his habit must be that of devotion, before he can take a delight in prayer. If you then make the outward worship ever so attractive, abridge it ever so much, adapt it as much as you can to the spirit of the age, if all this were even practicable: you would not have produced sentiments of devotion in those who resort to your synagogue or temple to hear you occasionally; the careless would not pray, for all your beautiful and pleasant method, for all your attraction of choir and organ, for all your harmonies and melodies, and he would go home cold and unimproved, although he had to listen to but a chapter of the Bible, and been entertained by an eloquent sermon which is based on human philosophy, and leaves faith and practice out of view. In other words, men must be devotional, before they can be devout in synagogue; and when this is attained, they will heartily join in prayer, respond respectfully to the blessings of the reader with a hearty "Amen," say with a sincere assent, "Holy, holy, holy is the Lord of hosts, the whole earth is full of his glory," and bow their head in reverence and thank God for all his goodness and mercy, which He has shown to each individual and his entire people Israel. And when the law is read four times every week in our assemblies, all present will listen attentively to each and every word, as though they stood again in the awful Presence at Sinai, and heard with their own ears the voice of the Almighty, announcing his august unalterable decrees in the immediate hearing of his people, as they follow the reader word by word, from a printed copy of the law which they have in their hand, in the Hebrew if they understand the holy language, and if not, in a translation, either German or English, or the various languages with which they are familiar, which have been supplied at all times by the teachers in Israel for the use of the people. Then comes fittingly, every Sabbath, a lecture* from one of the inspired writers and teachers whom our Father sent to us to enlighten us in his ways, and again we hear the admonition of these men calling us to hope and repentance; and then the service may close properly with a sermon from a minister in whom the people have confidence, whereby they will be exhorted to follow strictly what they have been taught by the words of the law and prophets; and then they can go home refreshed and improved by such an exercise, and become wiser and better, truly enlightened in the wisdom of God, knowing the way they should go.

The contrast between the two systems is too striking to require any farther illustration; for, on the one side there is self-glorification as the base of our assembling, on the other, the only feeling which can make our presence welcome in the eyes of God. If the first brings us hither, we had better stay at home; for no sanctification can result from it, and it is mockery to offer to God an insincere heart, where pride and not devotion has its seat. And if Israelites are only duly impressed with the sanctity of the house of God, with the proper idea of prayer, they will not exhibit that indecorum, that levity which is now

---

* The Haphtorah or section from the prophets.

justly complained of; there will be no time for talking, none for merriment, none for running in and out; and all will assemble at a proper time and stay till the service is ended, and demean themselves during the whole as servants before their master. Yes, the synagogue should be the place for prayer, the proper approach to the footstool of God. Come hither, you who are heavily laden with the cares and sorrows of life, on whom men look with disdain, who bear the scorn and persecution of the world: come hither, and ask of your God to give you his aid and protection, and you will issue forth strengthened by his spirit, and more able to bear cheerfully your sorrows and labours; yes, come hither and pray. And ye, too, who are laden with the burden of your sins, who feel that you have offended by deeds of wickedness your kind and benevolent Father, do not despair of his mercy and forgiveness; but come hither, and pour out before Him the anguish of your spirit, and look to Him for atonement and grace, because He is good and pardons iniquity; and issue hence, resolved to sin no more, strengthened by a new spirit of love and obedience; yes, come hither and pray.

Indeed, mere mechanical praying, to utter words without thought or feeling, is not what orthodoxy will sanction, not what Jewish religion requires. Do not, therefore, believe that we, who uphold the ancient order of things, are opposed to all improvement, or that we oppose reformers merely for the sake of party spirit: not so; we dread their inroads on the principles of faith and practice, or their leading people away from the true object of religion by dwelling so much on externals, as though the synagogue were the sum total of Judaism. Synagogue-going is certainly a duty; our wise men teach us that whoever attends not the house of God in his city is to be called a "bad neighbour:" all this is true; but it is only a means to an end, not the end itself. Good reforms may therefore be regarded as authorized, and consequently admissible; but those which are not, can never be legalized, though they might tend to fill the synagogue to overflowing, while under the ancient order it should stand empty and forsaken. If you accordingly want mere improvement, no orthodox will oppose you. For instance, the sale of the *Mitzvoth* in your congregation is an abuse; the reciting of money offerings on Sabbath, is a thing which should not exist: abolish both, and the sooner they are abolished the better; every day they exist is to continue so much longer an intolerable evil; and the loss to the revenue ought not to be considered of the least importance, as all they bring ought to be obtained by some other mode of finance. In this reform, I pledge you my word that all leaders of orthodoxy will go hand in hand with you, and applaud your abridging the service by the removal of such extraneous matters, which never had any business there. If you merely desire to leave out some useless poetical pieces, the *Piyutim*, which are in some respects unintelligible even to good Hebrew scholars; if you only require that the phraseology in some pieces should be altered to suit the altered state of the times; in short, if the intention is only to revise some portions of the prayer-book which are in themselves non-essential: ask, and I think that I can promise you, in the name of the principal teachers of the orthodox section, that your demands will be taken respectfully into consideration, and everything will be conceded which it is lawful to concede. Orthodoxy is not that unbending, unyielding, bigoted opposition to improvement which our opponents represent it; it understands perfectly well what the spirit of the age requires; but it can yield nothing to public clamour, nor to the demands which seekers of innovations may make to render Judaism a thing to accommodate itself to every phase of history. Such a religion would be none at all, as its ground would be constantly shifting; but to progress with the age, to adopt all the improvements which have been proved lawful, is perfectly within the limits of orthodoxy, and will therefore meet with no opposition from those who really love our religion.

But the reformers are not satisfied with this; "the prophets who wish to impose upon you the deceit of their own heart" will not improve merely; they wish to change, to revolutionize, to alter. They aver that Judaism is a very sick man, very sick indeed, and that this man must perish unless they come to his aid, with their medicines, with their university-purchased learning, drawn from sources which are unjewish in their nature and tendency. For my part, I do not think our religion is as sick as they represent it, consequently their aid is not needed. There are defects in practice; there is irreligion which stares us in the face; but this should be amended by our returning to first principles, not, however, by organic changes. Thus you teach your children to kiss* the *Sepher* as it is carried from and to the ark; all this is well

---

* A well-known custom in the German synagogues.

enough; but you ought to do more, you ought to impress them with the sacredness of the law, to teach them by a good example how to honour its precepts, and thus will you succeed in restoring among us a strict conformity of the old and young to the dictates of God, and remove the public disregard of the main duties even, which stamp us as Jews. But as for our modern doctors, we need them not, I boldly assert; if Judaism be sick now, as they maintain, it will perish, if they can slay it; if it have a little life, a small portion of vitality left, it will die outright, if their remedies be applied. No, no; our religion will not die; it is instinct with life, with undying strength, and it will resume its empire, notwithstanding the many doctors which now attempt its cure. But in very truth they are more likely to do mischief than good; they have done so whenever they have essayed their skill, and may the Guardian of Israel defend us against such physicians, against those who, if their advice be followed, will slay both the body and soul of our people. Still they maintain their views with so much perseverance, they assert their honesty so constantly that, notwithstanding our knowledge of their contemplated mischief, one is almost tempted to believe them sincere. They appeal so often to the judgment of the public, as though there were no wrong in their endeavours, enough almost to stagger their opponents. But we too wish to appeal to the same tribunal of publicity for our justification; we likewise do not dread to come before the people. In the ages of chivalry men could be summoned to a divine trial, to do some extraordinary feat to prove their innocence or the justice of their cause; if they succeeded in escaping unharmed, they were adjudged to be right, if otherwise, their guilt was supposed manifest. Or a man could be summoned into the lists to do battle for the justice of his cause, and only as victor could he establish that right was on his side. We have now indeed no such power to call back the age, when wager of battle was the arbiter between right and wrong, and the truth cannot be defended by carnal weapons; but we boldly challenge these false prophets, who teach you what the Lord has not said, to come with their arguments before the people, and we will meet them, and with the armour of truth we promise to overthrow their deceitful web of a vainglorious philosophy. If our religion is therefore sick, we must seek other remedies and other physicians, and they alone can bring us healing. That some sickness does exist, is evident from the clashing of sentiments which now prevails, from the hostile and angry position which one party assumes against the other; and hence it is but proper that we seek for the means of restoring a healthier tone than is now observable.

The remedy I would then recommend to you is EDUCATION. Here, before me [*pointing to the benches where the boys attending the congregational school were seated, with one teacher at each side*] I see your children, who are yet now in the ways of the world and its temptations; train them to know and fear God; encourage their teachers to instil in them daily the love of the Lord; strengthen the hands of God-fearing men to watch the avenues of their souls, that piety and religion may enter therein, and fortify them thus against the approach of iniquity. Should then the older branches even become forgetful of their duties, the new generation will arise and rebuild anew the temple of righteousness which their predecessors had desecrated. Yes, enlightened religion is that two-edged sword which destroys the enemies of Israel; it is potent against the assailants from without, and also against the teachers of error within our own camp. This instruction is the remedy, and through its means, through its blessed influence alone, can and will the deadly apathy which now chills us on the one side, and the dangerous counsels which threaten us on the other, be safely encountered and conquered. Who are those among you, who will cry out, "A sword for the Lord and Gideon," as did of old the handful of faithful undaunted warriors who followed their leader against the countless hosts of the sons of the East? Let these few, however few they be, arouse themselves to the contest, and victory must be with them; they will prevail, notwithstanding the struggle may be long and painful. But I really fear that few indeed are left, even here, who are not worshipping the idol of human pride in their heart. It is said, that there are seven thousand Jews in this city. But are there three hundred among them who could follow such a champion as Gideon into the battle, sure that God would be with them, because they had never bent their knee to human reason, to which all are now summoned to bow? Examine yourselves and say, How many are there here who have stood and stand unshaken amidst the conflict which now rages around us? I dread to think that I shall effect nothing by what I say to you to-day; I am almost sure that my words will die away unheeded by the vast majority of my hearers; but still I will speak and bear my testimony against the evil which is evident on all sides. I have been asked by your president to address you on the concerns of our religion; and, though I am sure that my plain speech will gain me but little favour, I must utter boldly the truth, careless whether I offend or not. And I now tell you that it would be wicked to use synagogue-reforms as the stepping-stone for a revolution in our religious system, which is contemplated by some; and that it would be unpardonable to transform the worship merely to render it pleasing to the ear. I do not assert that we should permit disorder and confusion in the recitation of the service, or suffer anything to obstruct uselessly the devotion which is offered in the house of God. Not so; the service can be read, if even it be not done so by all public readers, and should therefore be recited, in a manner to impress all with the sacredness of the places in which we are assembled, and to let them feel that what they utter is indeed prayer and thanksgiving. To do this, however, we require no change, no revolution. If on the contrary you lose sight of the true object of having synagogues, if you want them merely as places where you may periodically find entertainment, where you can spend an agreeable hour or two: I tell you, you would do much better to burn the synagogues, as they would not then be places which the presence of God can dwell in. So also in this ark is deposited the law, of which we read (in Deut. xxxi. 25–27): "And Moses commanded the Levites, the bearers of the ark of the covenant of the Lord, saying, Take this book of the law, and put it at the side of the ark of the covenant of the Lord your God, that it may remain there against thee for a witness. For I know thy rebellion, and thy stiff neck: behold, while I am yet alive with ye this day, ye have been rebellious against the Lord; and how much more after my death?" Here we see that the law was given us as a witness, to testify against us if we forsake its path. What then do you want with the law, if you become rebellious against it? What use is there to have a record of revelation, if you choose to elevate human reason as an arbiter of higher value than itself? If then this be your intention, if you mean to follow those who call on you to accept their dreams as your guide through life: *better burn the law*, than let it stand here forsaken, and its precepts neglected. Yes, let fire consume the synagogues if they cease to receive those who worship God; better that we have no law, that the pure fire should consume the books which contain it, than that we should cast away its obligation while we hold it in our hands.

But it depends upon the people to step in to arrest the evil. If the shepherds will not feed you on the pastures of faith, follow not their lead, abandon them to their own conceit, and do you pursue the plain letter of the religion of your forefathers. Ay, it is an evil, that those who ought to be led should watch their leaders: still, if the times demand it, if it appears that those, who should march before you with sound precepts and a good example, use their influence to elevate themselves above the people, abandon them, and, relying on the guidance of our Father which has never forsaken Israel, march onward in the simplicity of your hearts, safer in your ignorance than with such men's learning. Listen not, therefore, to any advice which would sever your connexion with the masses of Jacob's sons, and regard with suspicion the introduction of new doctrines, and watch well that no unbelief takes root in your hearts. Reflect that sincerity is the touchstone of the value of your words and deeds; and for this reason you must be very circumspect, that you guard against the propagation of any ideas which are against the well-established doctrines, which have inspired for so many centuries hope and trust in the hearts of the oppressed descendants of Abraham. Here I hold in my hand the form of prayers, in accordance with which we have for many centuries past offered up our devotions, whether in synagogue or in our houses, whether on land or at sea, whether amidst civilized nations or savage hordes. The ideas this old book [*holding up the prayer-book*] contains, and the precepts and doctrines which are embraced in this holy volume [*placing his hands on a Hebrew Bible which the speaker had before him*] have become incorporated with the very being of Israel, and are in truth the guiding-star of every act of their life. The words, therefore, of our prayers, are not merely a frivolous thing, but the very life-breath of the Israelite's existence. But if you say, "Blessed art thou, O Lord! who revivest the dead," and believe it not; if you say, "And to Jerusalem thy city mayest thou speedily return," and believe it not; if you say, "The plant of David thy anointed do thou cause speedily to grow," and believe it not; if you say, "Blessed art thou, O Lord, who causest thy glory to return to Zion," and believe it not: you are liars and hypocrites. For in truth, if you pretend to give your assent to such holy ideas in the prayers you utter, and then reject them as not in consonance with human reason, that idol to which you mean to subject all your precepts and doctrines: you are liars and hypocrites! These are harsh words to utter; but would you have me palliate the woful sin thus committed? would you desire that, instead of unveiling the hideous deformity of such vile deception, it should be glossed over and screened by honeyed expressions? Not this was the practice of the ancient prophets of truth, whom the Lord wisely sent to speak in his behalf. And if the picture is so dreadful and hideous, so that even its proper name will offend: how necessary is it then to fly from the reality, and to endeavour to remove it as far as possible from our midst!

No, friends, the prayers are the expression of the long-cherished hopes of our ancient people; they never could have originated except from the conviction that they are actually based upon the revelation of God, and therefore alone fit to be addressed to Him in every circumstance and at all times. But this consideration again forces upon us to suffer no sacrilegious hand to tear asunder this unseen, yet ever-felt bond which unites our people so strongly together in one faith and one hope, which is the same wherever we are found, in all our wanderings; and whoever teaches to the contrary does not speak in accordance with the truth, which is contained for us in the Bible, the record of God's will. Our prayers, you must reflect, are not petitions which men invented, but such requests and such praises as are founded on the Scriptures, and are frequently in the very words of the Bible. To consign them, therefore, to oblivion, is to contradict the teaching of the divine record: and how are we to adopt in lieu of these scriptural prayers the varying productions of the passing age, which change with every season? Let those do so who see not in our religion a perennial, undying system, whose hope is not firmly placed on the Lord God of Israel. For our part, we should not alone have the feelings which the promises of Scripture inspire us with, but we should express them by outward words, by prayer and thanksgiving, in accordance with the standard of right and truth; and then we shall have an unvarying guide, which we can follow without the least danger of straying from the proper path; and we shall be able to bid defiance to all erroneous teaching, come from what source it may, when they who mean to mislead us do not speak in the spirit of revelation, but endeavour to impose on us the deceit of their own hearts, and their dreams, whether drawn from a false philosophy, or a heated imagination, or a bold infidelity; for we shall be protected with the armour of proof, against which all assaults will be in vain.

But it is time that I draw to a conclusion; I have detained you long by the remarks which you have so patiently listened to, and I regret deeply that I had to use the language of invective instead of words of gentle persuasion. But when the evil is imminent, it were weakness and folly to use sweet phrases; whereas the conscience should be awakened and sinfulness sternly rebuked. You may think me unjust; many no doubt will do it; but I have nothing to ask for myself; it is the duty of those who proclaim the word of God, of those to whom He has given the power of speech, to regard their mission, not their interest; and hence, when denunciation is needed, let them use bold language, relying on the aid of their God whose messengers they are. But how happy would it be for all of us, if the spirit of godliness were again to spread anew among us; no one would rejoice more than the one who now so bitterly inveighs against the sins of the age, were piety to triumph over all obstacles, and divine knowledge become universal among all Israel, in the words of the father of the prophets: "Who would grant that all the people of the Lord might be prophets, that the Lord might put his spirit on them." With these words do I end, in the fervent hope that you all may be enlightened in God's wisdom, and be led to seek for instruction in his law: so that ye may all be acceptable in his presence, when you are summoned to Him to receive the reward of your acts in this life. Amen.

NOTE. It may appear a piece of vanity to write out from memory the extemporaneous remarks, without a single note having been prepared, which were delivered in the Broadway Synagogue, at Cincinnati, during a brief visit there, on the 28th of April, 5615. But even before I left that city, I found that some at least had misunderstood me, and said that I had made assertions without proof, and merely scolded the people and their teachers, without adducing any arguments for my assertion. For my ownself, it is a matter of perfect indifference what may be said there or elsewhere; during a public life of near twenty-six years it has never come into my mind to refrain expressing my opinions for fear of not receiving much praise or reward of any kind. But far different is it where the cause one defends is at stake; I ventured in the lions' den and bearded them where they are all-powerful, and I equally powerless. To do this then ineffectually, or with inadequate weapons, would not have been alone folly, but wickedness likewise; for, if the truth could not be properly defended by such as myself, the advocacy of it ought to have been left to other and abler tongues. This consideration has moved me to do what I have but seldom done, spread before my readers the above speech so far as I could recollect it. As there were about eight hundred, or perhaps near a thousand persons in the synagogue to listen to me, they can decide whether anything has been altered in the argument or manner from what they heard themselves; no one would suppose that I would make any changes or suppress anything which I advanced orally; in fact, I have endeavoured to give back the very words I used, although it cannot be expected that this can be possible in all respects, after the lapse of six weeks. Approximation is all that can be reached, and all that is needed.—*From the Occident of July,* 5615.

DISCOURSE VI.

GOD SPOKE.*

FRIENDS AND BRETHREN!

We celebrate this day the most stupendous event which ever occurred since the creation of the world, if it does not exceed it in importance to all living on the earth. It was on this day that our forefathers stood before Mount Sinai, and heard the word of the living God speaking to them from the midst of the fire, when He, by his wisdom, gave a new life to their spirit, and endowed them with the power to know and fear Him all their days. Yes, it was to teach us how to regard Him, that God came down in his glory, in order that we might be free from false conceptions respecting the Being who is the Lord of all; that we might revere Him who is the God of Israel! But

---

* Substance of a sermon delivered at Baltimore, in the Portuguese Synagogue, on the first day of Pentecost, 5617.

who is He whom we thus acknowledge? tell us, ye wise in worldly wisdom, do you know Him? Were a painter to conceive the most beautiful, the most perfect, the most enchanting and glorious picture: could he represent to us an image of God? No,—his art would be in vain; he could not reach the elevation of the Holy One. Were a sculptor to labour with all the intensity of genius, and produce before us a work of surpassing grandeur and sublimity, of proportions the most exact, and of a vastness hitherto unapproached: would this be a representation of our God? O no; it would be a weak embodiment of human ideas, unworthy of the One whom nothing can equal. Perhaps the poet may picture in his glowing language the outlines of the Almighty, and bring before our imagination a sketch of the highest idea, so that we could say that nothing can surpass this: would this represent to us the God of Israel? No, friends; it would still be only human imagining, but no realization of what God is. But high and holy as He is, He dwells within us and around us; in all the earth there are evidences of his glory and might; and "in whatever place He permits us to mention his name, there will He come unto us and bless us." For equally little as the painter, the sculptor, and the poet can represent Him before us, so little can the architect erect a house fit for his glory. Imagine a temple ever so grand,—imagine the pride of the world, the house restored by Herod, which erst graced the hill of Moriah, and to which our fathers made their pilgrimage three times every year, and which, alas! is now laid waste and ruined,—imagine this glorious structure infinitely more resplendent than it was: it would still not be commensurate with the majesty of the God and King of Israel! Columns, and halls, though fit expressions of human feelings, contain not the Being whom we worship; and He dwells no less in the humblest meeting-houses, where we assemble to call on Him, even here, in this temporary synagogue where we have met to-day to invoke his Name, than in the most majestic of structures; and He will not be absent from the midst of his adorers to bless them with his spirit. And He whom the world cannot contain, in whom all exists, "He, the Holy One, dwelleth amidst the praises of Israel." Wisely has the Psalmist said תהלות ישראל "the *praises*," not in hymns, chaunts, or songs, which may proceed from efforts of art, carefully put together in moments of deliberation, and coldly calculated for effect, but in heartfelt issues of thanksgiving, where the spirit utters what it feels; it is there that God dwells; it is there that the universal Father deigns to be present to be invoked, to be adored, to bless those who call on Him. Who, then, is the God of Israel? Even the Creator of the universe, the embodiment of all the powers which we can conceive to exist, the Author and Originator of everything, and without whom nothing could be.

This is the adored One presented to us in the Scriptures, and in his name are we assembled this day to commemorate the event which gave us the light in which we might walk securely. Let us then take for our contemplation two remarkable passages of the Scriptures, the first words of the first book of Moses, בראשית ברא אלהים, "In the beginning God created" (Gen. i. 1), and the introduction to the Ten Commandments, וידבר אלהים, "And God spoke" (Exod. xx. 1). If the Bible contained nothing besides these two sentences, we should have enough to be thankful for, that the Lord gave us knowledge, through his revelation, of the great truths thus announced, namely, that He created the world, and that He spoke to us audibly, and thus imparted to us a knowledge of his will. First, as regards the announcement that God is the Creator. All men are willing to acknowledge that they are of themselves powerless, can produce nothing, and cannot destroy any substance which exists. Some, nevertheless, imagine that nature always existed, and that from the elements, as they were from eternity, the earth and its system were gradually developed. To obviate this idea the Bible says, "In the beginning God created." When it entered into the will of the Cause of causes to call forth the universe, He was alone in his power and glory; and He then produced by his mere word the substance of the material world from the waste state of non-existence. It was in the beginning, the first origin of things, that this took place, and then אלהים "*Elohim,*" the Possessor of all the collective powers imaginable, the Almighty, unaided, unprompted, without compulsion, without advice, created whatever He deemed fitting to make; and just as He willed this, and not otherwise, was it done; and just as his wisdom designed, so was all established. Here, then, you have the nature of God, as far as he has revealed himself to us. He was the First, before all things were; and He was the Originator, when the universe was made. But this is not all which the words of our text teach us. To man exertion is fatiguing, labour exhausts his powers, and when his time of toil has passed over him, he is compelled to rest, and is no longer able to continue his work. Not so the Creator; He called into being the substance of things, the vast elements from which natural bodies are compounded; yet his might was not thereby lessened, and He continued in the undiminished possession of all the attributes of majesty and power which He had before. It was God, the all-powerful, who created, and all-sufficient He remained, and his creative spirit pervaded the mass He had produced, and He endowed it with light and life, and enabled it to become organized, beautified, and adorned by the same potent word which had first made it. And God said, "Let there be light;" and barely had the thought become word, than the word saw itself accomplished, and darkness fled from where it had rested on the face of the deep, and light spread itself over every part of the creation. The Creator, therefore, is not merely the Author of a lifeless, dark, shapeless mass, but also of all the light, beauty, order, and harmony which everywhere greet us in the remotest recesses of all the boundless space.

Yet even with this the attributes of God are not completed. There are practical atheists who imagine that, with the creation, the work of the Lord on earth has ceased. He is too vast, too far removed, too great, too holy, to take cognizance of what is wrought here below; we are thus left to work our own will, to amuse ourselves as we may deem proper, and there is no accountability, no punishment, because there is no Judge. "God hath forsaken the earth," so do men often say: "it is enough for us that we believe that we did not produce what is around us; but there is no need that we look for counsel and advice to any source save our reason." These, however, are told, "In the beginning *God* created," meaning He, the Creator, is the Source of the power that animates all; He is therefore and necessarily the same who sustains all; for who is there to whom He has transferred his godhead? And if He is the Preserver, He must also be the Ruler; for to whom has He surrendered the dominion? who is there to dispute with Him the supervision and control over all the beings? And as He thus rules, He cannot be indifferent to the acts of his creatures; since he must have made them for ulterior happiness, which is proved by the innumerable springs of delight and enjoyment which everywhere diffuse gladness and pleasure, by the innumerable forms of beauty and symmetry which in all times and places enchant the vision,—in brief, by all the contrivances which administer to the wants of man. And if He superintends the work that is done everywhere, He must also take cognizance of all the deeds which may militate against the well-being of those whom He has made for happiness, and visit them with his displeasure, and check the injury they may be intended to inflict. Israel's God, therefore, is not a mere abstraction, an Author of nature and nature's laws, which are left to work out a certain amount of phenomena and effects, both physical and moral; not one who, having made what He pleased, left his creatures without control, subject only to their own impulses to work out their will and pleasure, and to rule wherever their rude power might prevail; on the contrary, He is still here to restrain and to punish, to superintend and to reward; and so He will continue to the end of time; and all this because He is "*Elohim*," God all-powerful, unchanging, all-sufficient, and not subject to the control of aught which He has made. Nature indeed is the child of God; the laws which govern her are firmly established, and not to be checked, controlled, or modified by any act of ours; yet they are submissive to his word and thought, and are constantly ready to obey his will. They, like ourselves, are amenable to his power only, and therefore our responsibility is not lessened by the admitted fact, that outward nature is acted on by uniform laws and checks which no creature can transgress. But instead of this removing us from God's supervision, it only brings us the closer under his eye; for He, who instituted all we see, will not need to exert any doubtful or uncertain power to regard us each and all with a special providence: we are always under his view, and cannot escape from his cognizance, let us flee whither we may; in the most open and in the most secret place we are alike under the eye of the unchanging, omniscient Father; "for, behold, He slumbereth not, He sleepeth not, the Guardian of Israel;" and we are always remembered, always guarded, always protected, just as we are constantly held accountable in every stage of our existence.

It is not necessary to point out to you, in the various stages of the progress of the world, that these ideas have been verified; to us there has been no change; to the divinely enlightened mind there has been no transfer of power, and the same God who created in the beginning, is still here in this world to rule and govern as his wisdom may dictate. But with the creation of matter his work was not yet accomplished;

He indeed had given us reason, by which we could in a measure judge between right and wrong, or rather between what responded to what is agreeable, and what is obnoxious to us. But the absolute knowledge of what is right and wrong was not inherent in man, or else there could have been no difference of opinion in regard to morals and duty. He, therefore, who held us accountable for our deeds, would have acted unjustly, had He left this uncertain guide, unaided human reason, to be the only arbiter in matters in which all men are alike concerned, where the views of one, however honestly entertained, may work injury to another. Besides all which, we have undoubted evidence that those who had to rely on their own investigations for light, progressed slowly and painfully, and found themselves still far from their goal at which they had been aiming. Justice and mercy are, however, the attributes of God, no less than power and sovereignty. He therefore made, from the earliest ages of the world, his will known to mankind, that they might have a knowledge of the way which they should go. But the government of the passions was more in consonance with the ideas which the early descendants of man entertained, and they refused to be guided by the divine counsels which would restrain their inclinations and direct them to higher objects. It was then that there arose the ancestor of our race, and in him the truth found a refuge, and he taught his children how to fear the Lord. And when those who sprung from Abraham were subjected to bondage and cruel labour, their cause was not forgotten by God, and He sent his servant Moses to break asunder their chains, and to lead them forth to freedom. But what would a mere bodily freedom have been worth? a simple release from thraldom, if their spirit had yet remained captive to the idols of Egypt? Nothing permanent; and a slavish mind could readily have succumbed to the power of other tyrants, and wrong and oppression would have been multiplied as before. But God remembered his covenant with Abraham, Isaac, and Jacob; and, in redeeming their posterity from Egyptian servitude, he made them also worthy to enjoy freedom, by liberating their spirit from the slavery of the passions. This great event, the manifestation of the evident glory of God, was accordingly witnessed by all our forefathers; and men, women, and children, the bond and the free, the man-servants and maid-servants, and the strangers who were among them, were brought to the foot of Sinai, in the third month after their going out of Egypt; and there they heard the words of the living God speaking to them audibly and clearly all that He had ordained for their spiritual freedom.

Let us pause here. The words again are וידבר אלהים, "And God spoke." The same infinite Being who created the world, the *Elohim*, the embodiment of all the powers which can exist, who alone called forth the universe out of nothing, now appeared in his majesty before the eyes of his redeemed people; and though they saw no similitude, the likeness of anything which they could imitate, they all heard the same voice, at the same time, in the same manner, rising clear and loud above the din of convulsed nature, and it sunk deeply into their soul, never thereafter to be forgotten, not even when drawing their dying breath. And indeed it was almost the moment of their dissolution; the fear of personal danger overwhelmed the stoutest; and while their spirit hovered thus on the confines of eternity, the words of the Everlasting One were engraved in their very heart, and they went forth enlightened and strong; and the light thus kindled has never since been quenched, and it has burnt brightly notwithstanding the many tribulations through which they had to pass. No nation had ever heard before them the voice of the living God, and they started back in awe and dread; but they were told that it was only in order that the fear of God might ever be upon them, that they had been permitted to see and hear what no one before or since has been privileged to do; and thus they were initiated into the covenant of life, and, endowed with this knowledge and imperishable wisdom, they have pursued their mission to this day. And it was God who spoke; not a delegate of the highest power, not a mediator, to stand between the Creator and the creature, not even a messenger who was sent to tell what he had alone been permitted to hear; but all the people heard the living God, the same who was one at the creation, when first the light came forth out of darkness; the same whom Abraham adored; the same who had promised his protection to Jacob, who had thus far guided them unscathed amidst the nations of the earth; and He taught them all without a mediator, without a second to aid Him, without a superior to teach Him wisdom, and they felt then and thus that He alone is the Lord, and there is none beside Him.

The words also which thus proceeded from the

mouth of eternal Wisdom were worthy of their Source. They are clear and defined; they exhibit us the Creator as our Benefactor, who alone has the government of all that exists; who demands of man to adore Him alone, since there is no other being who can save when He intends to punish, who can prevent Him from blessing when He desires to bestow his favour. We are also told that we must not expect to be indulged with impunity when we dare to rebel against our Sovereign; we are certified that He is a jealous God, ay, jealous, loving his children, solicitous for their welfare, and He will therefore not tolerate that, degrading their reason, and forgetful of their allegiance to their King, their love to their Father, their gratitude to their Benefactor, they should render homage to the conceptions of human reason or folly, which have been in all times set up as divinities or tutelary powers to screen man from the immediate vengeance, or to propitiate the favour of God. We were taught to regard the Lord as He is, independent in his being, and uncontrolled in his power; wherefore we would be untrue to our trust, if we associated with Him any conceivable thing, be it a reality or fiction, in the adoration due to Him alone. And it is worthy of the character of the Most Holy, that He should visit with his indignation such a delinquency; since it would tend to bring error with all its baleful train of misery, which it was the object of the promulgation of the law at Sinai to destroy forever. The moral laws which were imparted have proved themselves, after centuries of experience, such that nothing has been devised which could in the least add to their truth and beauty; and they are as applicable on this day, as at the first manifestation of the Lord's glory on Horeb. And the law has remained the inheritance of our race, and we have carried it with us in all our wanderings, and notwithstanding our frequent transgressions we have never departed from it altogether; but some have remained faithful, when the many cast aside their allegiance. And it is thus that we have preserved the knowledge of the "*Elohim*" who created the world in the beginning, who gave us reason and freedom of will, by which we might labour to please Him, and who, as a just and watchful Guardian, expects of us to enrich ourselves with good deeds,—but who is also the same "*Elohim*" who came himself to enlighten our reason, that we might know the deeds we should fulfil, and the work we should accomplish to merit his mercy and kindness. It is therefore not proper for us to select what may please our fancy, and reject what is not suitable to our taste; for we are told, "And God spoke *all* these words," they all are his decrees, the expression of his will; and the whole must therefore claim our obedience and our entire acquiescence. There is no difference between one word and the other; and "Remember the Sabbath day to keep it holy" is to be regarded with the same deep veneration as "Thou shalt not murder; thou shalt not commit adultery; thou shalt not steal." And the duties which concern our relation to God alone will have, when obeyed, the same beneficial effect on us, as those which relate to the well-being of society; and as we find the Creator still with his power undiminished, wisdom undecayed, and mercy unchanged, our obedience should be likewise undiminished, undecayed, and unchanged. Ages have not altered our relation to God; and the existence of our political state, or its decay, should therefore have no influence on us, to absolve us in the least of all practicable duties which the law of God has prescribed for us. We are still the same to whom the divine legislation was first imparted; we are still the same descendants from the Patriarchs that we always were; we are still the people chosen from all nations to testify by our presence to the Unity of God; and we have the same means that we always had to prove our faith and trustworthiness, by obeying the commandments which have been imparted to us. Let us then show that we are worthy of this high destiny; that we are willing to continue faithful to our mission; that we truly believe in the God of Israel, who is not a mere abstraction, a divinity without power, without vigilance, without providence, without justice, but a reality, who has created, who governs, who judges, because He has given us a law which will instruct and guide us in all our earthly relations, and point out to us the way which will infallibly lead us to the portals of everlasting life. But to do this, we must be active in our testimony, not content ourselves with words and mere profession, but continue to obey all the words which God, the Elohim Creator, has spoken; and then will He come among us in his all-pervading glory, whenever and wherever we are met to mention his Name, even in our humble place of assembly, or wherever He is invoked amidst the praises of Israel, and bless us with his spirit and with his light, which is life everlasting. Amen.

DISCOURSE VII.

OUR CONSOLATION.

BRETHREN AND FRIENDS! After darkness comes light, and after tribulations, enlargement; so do we Israelites also turn, after the fast which is kept in memory of the destruction of the temple and for the people of the Lord that fell by the sword, with confidence and trust to the hope of consolation and redemption which are to compensate us for the trials which we have had to encounter, during so many wars, in which we twice lost our country and sanctuary, and in the subsequent persecutions which we had to endure during our wanderings among all the nations of the earth. Let us then take for the subject of our to-day's contemplation the commencement of the fortieth chapter of the prophecies of Isaiah. After he had in the preceding chapters spoken of punishment and retribution as the result of sinning, he opens with the words:

נחמו נחמו עמי יאמר אלהיכם:

"Comfort ye, comfort ye my people, saith your God. Speak ye (comfort) to the heart of Jerusalem, and cry unto her, that her time (of sorrow) is accomplished, that her iniquity is pardoned; for she hath received of the hand of the Lord twofold for all her sins."

The prophet says, that they should be comforted who are God's people. But were these the men of his own day? Assuredly not; for he lived in the time of Ahaz, a king renowned for his wickedness, who, after he had been to Damascus where he had seen an altar of heathenism which suited his fancy, ordered his high-priest in Jerusalem to erect him one exactly like it in the court of the Lord, whereas he removed the altar built by Solomon to the north side thereof, and ordered all the sacrifices to be brought on his new structure, while that consecrated to God was to be only occasionally visited at the king's pleasure. Such a prince and such a generation were not to be styled God's people, *'Ammi;* for he emphatically announced through another of his messengers, that a nation, as the Israelites were then, are properly *Lo-'Ammi*, not my people, "for you are not my people, and I will not belong to you." Yea, Isaiah himself had already said to them in his first chapter: "Your new-moons and your appointed feasts my soul hateth; they have become a burden unto me; I am weary to bear them." And just before this he exclaimed: "When ye come to appear in my presence—who hath required this at your hand to tread down my courts?" The worship of such a people with their festivals and prayers, their coming in masses to God's threshold, were all regarded as a burden too heavy to be borne by the Lord; and can it be, then, to such as these that the prophet applied the term *'Ammi*, my people, speaking on behalf of the Most High? No, brethren, it was not that generation who could claim affinity to God; they were not his people, and the decree had gone forth that they should be banished from the temple and the land which they polluted by their abominations; their sin was to be visited with expulsion and slaughter, and no comfort was to be given to those who forsook their Father. But Isaiah did not speak to those who then heard him; he looked far down into the depths of futurity, and there discovered quite another people of Israel, of whom Zephaniah spoke when he said: "And I will leave as a remnant in the midst of thee an afflicted and poor people, and they will trust in the name of the Lord. The remnant of Israel will do no wrong, and will not speak falsehood, and there shall not be found in their mouth the tongue of deceit." It is such as these who are called, as Hosea said, "The children of the living God," instead of being formerly known as *Lo-'Ammi*, whom the Lord will not look upon as his people. What was not then in Jerusalem, therefore, the prophet foresaw as sure to arise, centuries after his time, perhaps centuries after our own days: and he says in the name of the Lord, that to this holy people, to those whom God will call his own, there should be spoken comfort, there should be brought a renewed hope, that of a time of sorrow at an end, of sin atoned for, of a period of perfect reconciliation to the Creator, with as much certainty as the destruction would be, which was so soon to overtake those who had become rebels against the law of Heaven.

That the consolation thus promised has not yet taken place, is evident from the records of history; there has never been a time since Isaiah spoke, that our nation presented that devotion and union in the interest of their faith, to be entitled to the high distinction which the name of *'Ammi*, God's people, confers on them: especially if we should assume, as some modern critics pretend to believe, that that part of the book of Isaiah, commencing with the fortieth chapter, was written after the rebuilding of the temple in the time of Zerubbabel. Instead of such an hypothesis weakening our position, it would make it the stronger; as surely during no period of the duration of the second temple, had we much of consolation to boast of; first subject to the Persians; then to the Greeks; again a brief period of independence, which was soon completely lost through the ambition of men who should have been content with the priesthood, and who finally called in the Romans to settle their senseless quarrels, through which means the state and people sunk finally before the assaults of the dangerous arbitrators, who had first appeared as their friends. We therefore ask, when was it proclaimed within the streets of Jerusalem, that her iniquity had been atoned for? when, that her time of sorrow was ended? You appeal in vain to any history; it never took place; but its accomplishment is nevertheless certain, though the time may be far distant yet. Look at the construction of the sentence; if we translate the Hebrew literally, it is not as we have given it, "saith your God," but it is אמר, meaning "He will say" at the time when it is to be done, and then will He say to his messenger, to speak this comfort to those who are *his* people, to those who are worthy to be called by his Name, that they will then have atoned for all their previous faults, and that then a new and better era will arise for them. But let us next see what the words of consolation are which will be addressed to God's people. We find them in verses six, seven, and eight, as follows: "A voice saith, Proclaim; and he saith, What shall I proclaim? All flesh is grass, and all its goodliness as the flower of the field; the grass withereth, the flower fadeth, because the breath of the Lord hath blown upon it; surely the people is grass. The grass withereth, the flower fadeth, but the word of our God will stand forever." This is what will be said; but what sort of consolation is this for Israel? It is simply the assurance that, let occur what may, let all on earth perish, there is one thing alone which will survive, and this is the Word of our God, even his revelation which is with us, and his spirit which has been planted in us. In the spring the grass comes out of the ground, when the winter's snows have melted away; and as the season advances, many beautiful flowers cover the surface of the ground, emblems of the Creator's mercy and goodness. But scarcely has a day elapsed, and the wind of the Lord has passed over the flowery meads, when the grass is dried up, and the flowers hang languidly, withering on their stalks. We speak of earthly prosperity, of fortune and pleasure which accompany many of those we call happy; but we turn again to behold them, when we see them withered and faded, and their joy turned into grief and mourning; for "surely the people is grass," and nothing can stand before the indignation of the Lord, and what men build falls before the blast of his breath. His Word, however, which He spoke thousands of years ago, has survived all that ever existed, and will stand, outlasting all forever, just as He himself is imperishable. Error has been promulgated by men of our nation no less than others; enemies have assailed the word of God, to cause Israel to forget their allegiance; but one after the other have they had to retire from their vain contest; and what we have been taught as the truth has triumphed, and it exists as strong as in the beginning. And though we may see these enemies of truth wealthy and powerful, enjoying robust health and revelling in pleasure; though even we may see their followers increase, and that to appearance their ideas obtain constantly new adherents: let us not despair of the cause which has been intrusted into our hands. We indeed may behold how the wicked flourish like the grass, and grow in beauty like the flower; but we may rest assured, that there are pains and sorrows which are concealed from the eye of man, and which, nevertheless, may and will afflict those who have rebelled against the word of God. For we read in Isaiah lxvi. 24: "And they shall go forth and look upon the carcasses of the men that have transgressed against me; for their worm shall not die, and their fire shall not be quenched; and they shall be an abhorrence unto all flesh." We are not the judges of the Lord; we can, therefore, not determine why all things around us are just as we find them; we have not the means of forming a proper opinion of the connexion of the different events which constantly occur. But the time will come, when it will be made known who has been the Lord's, and who has earned his approbation, and who it is that has been brought into his holy presence; and who again it is whom He has condemned to the shade of his displeasure; and then will men go forth, and have positive evidence of the torments of those who, knowing their Creator, have wilfully transgressed against Him (הפשעים בי); for indeed their worm, the internal remorse which will perpetually gnaw at their spirit, will not die; their wrongdoing will ever be with them, the consciousness of their wickedness will not leave them for a moment, and the fire of their punishment will burn with a never-failing flame, a flame self-fed, constantly burning, never quenched; because they have misled others to iniquity, and perpetuated their evil in those who follow their example; and thus they shall be an abhorrence to all flesh; all will recognize that their doom is just, and they will rejoice that they did not yield to the impulse of their desire to follow the sinners on their path of rebellion.

Our consolation therefore is, "The word of our God will stand forever." It is accordingly in this, in the law of God, in the word of his prophets, in the teachings which the men inspired by Him have left us, where we must seek for comfort, and where we shall discover the things which will befall us. How many misfortunes have not passed over our nation; and yet we are here, to testify by our presence that we are still unconsumed. All the efforts made to extinguish our name have only resulted in diminishing our numbers, but never in destroying us altogether. And whenever we went astray from the law of God, and endeavoured to become like other men, we were not permitted to accomplish our design, and we were retained in the service of the One who had chosen us as his messengers. It was his law which, itself surviving all on earth, has preserved us also, and we are here to-day to declare our adherence to Him, as we yesterday deposited another copy* of the law in the

---

* On the evening preceding, a new copy of the Torah had been brought to the synagogue, with appropriate ceremony and an ad-

ark that it might testify for us, that we still faithfully preserve the letter of the Scripture, that it may guide us on our path. And when we regard our state of dispersion, our *Galuth* all over the earth, submitting as we necessarily do to the laws of the various states which divide the government of the globe among them, we must not despair of the future of Israel, nor be led to imagine that this will always remain so; since for us a change is coming, sure though tardy, when Israel will again be a united people, with a government and laws of their own. For so we read in the *law of Moses* (Deut. xxx. 1–5): "And it shall come to pass when all these things are come upon thee, the blessing and the curse, which I have set before thee, and thou callest them to mind among all the nations, whither the Lord thy God hath driven thee; so that thou returnest unto the Lord thy God, and hearkenest unto his voice according to all that I command thee this day, thou and thy children, with all thy heart and with all thy soul,—that the Lord thy God will restore thy captivity, and have compassion upon thee; and He will again gather thee from all the nations, whither the Lord thy God hath scattered thee. If thy outcasts be at the outermost parts of heaven, from there will the Lord thy God gather thee, and from there will He take thee; and the Lord thy God will bring thee into the land which thy fathers possessed, and thou shalt possess it; and He will do thee good, and multiply thee above thy fathers." If words mean anything, it is stated here, as distinctly as pos-

---

dress in German by the writer of this, of which, however, no memoranda have been preserved.

sible, that the state of dispersion of Israel will one day cease, and that the children of Abraham, Isaac, and Jacob will form again a state of their own in no other country than the land of Palestine, whither they were about to pass when Moses pronounced this remarkable prophecy. It is not for me to assert positively, that *all* Israelites will dwell in our ancient heritage; perhaps many may continue to reside in various countries, and only go up once a year or oftener to observe the national feasts with their brothers, in the city where the Lord will let his glory dwell again as of yore. But whether this be so or not, we have the assurance that the main seat of the nation, and of the national worship, will be where it was in the time of our prosperity, under David and Solomon, in the identical land of Israel, which will then be accessible through the new means of intercommunication to persons residing on all the earth, within the circle of every year. But the time is not specified by the prophet; it all depends on the return of the people to righteousness, "Even this day, if you will hearken to my voice," (Psalm xcv. 7), as the verse is explained by our wise men, meaning, that every day is the period of redemption, if the people will but sincerely repent, and obey the voice of God with all their heart and with all their soul.

It may be asked, How will this repentance be brought about? We have not the means to answer the question with precision; but we may assume that it can take place even without a direct miraculous agency of God. There is constantly going forward a change in the manner of thinking and acting of mankind at large; however we may complain of an occasional retrogression, there is evidently a point unto which the mind of man is tending, and which it will ultimately reach, notwithstanding the many disturbing causes to which it has always been subjected. We may therefore maintain that, in the process of time, the mind of Israelites may be so imbued with the vanity of all they have hitherto been clinging to, they will so thoroughly discover the folly of all the objects they have been pursuing, that they will with one accord turn to the law of God, and seek in that for the course of life they should pursue, and thus they will literally return to the Lord their God with all their heart and all their soul; and thus, being again worthy of his favour, they will be fit to be united into one nation, and to re-occupy the rank of an independent people, a model and light to all others.

That the words of Moses can bear no other interpretation than that which they evidently convey, needs no argument; they are too distinct and too direct to require any elucidation; unbelief may indeed step in and deny their truths; but this is all it can accomplish, it cannot interpret them to mean anything else than the simple announcement, that the outcasts of Israel are to be gathered from all the places of their dispersion, to be united again into one people, ruled by the law of God, under circumstances which will render it forever respected and obeyed. Not alone, however, will our own people be benefitted by this restoration; for we are told in Isaiah, "That from Zion shall go forth the law, and the word of the Lord from Jerusalem." The truth shall radiate from the centre, where it will have taken up its abode, and it will illuminate the pathway of all nations; for they will also desire to walk in the paths of the Lord, after they have learned some of his ways; and as Israel has acquired faith in the law of God, so will all others cling to the same, that they may know how to regulate their course of life.

The means to accomplish this may be perfectly in the course of nature; events may gradually tend to bring all men irresistibly to one mode of thinking, and thus pave the way for the triumph of truth. But there will also be another more active and direct agency employed to effect the will of the Creator. Just as He sent his servant Moses to become the deliverer and legislator of Abraham's descendants when they sighed under Egyptian bondage, thus will He send another messenger to effect his purpose with regard to Israel in the first instance, and afterwards to the rest of the world. In other words, we expect a bodily messenger, a direct agent of the Lord, in the manner as Moses was, and this personage is known as the Messiah, or God's anointed; and of him we read in Isaiah xi. 1, 2, "And there shall come forth a shoot out of the stem of Jessé, and a sprout shall spring out of his roots. And there shall rest upon him the spirit of the Lord, the spirit of wisdom and understanding, the spirit of counsel and might, the spirit of knowledge and of the fear of the Lord." It is needless to recite for you the whole chapter of which these verses are the introduction; read it for yourselves, and you will find that it exactly agrees with the prediction of Moses regarding the assemblage of the dispersed of Israel, with the sole addition that, what is given in Deuteronomy as merely impending, is here connected with a special agent, who is to be a descendant from David, the king of Israel. The prophecy is enlarged, not limited, the event is connected with an agent, and such a one as will be in every wise suited for the task which he is to accomplish. Wisdom, knowledge, intelligence, and above all the fear of the Lord, are to be his distinguishing characteristics; strength of mind and of body is to mark him as the first among men, guided by an unerring spirit of divine intelligence, which is to animate him, as it did the prophets of old. What may not such a person effect, even were the course of things to follow the natural channel, at a time when intelligence shall have progressed to the point of discovering that opinions hitherto cherished were all vain and idle? But we are assured also in another passage, that just "as at the time we went forth from Egypt would God show us his miracles;" wherefore we have the fullest confidence that every thing, the natural and supernatural, will combine to forward the will of God on earth; and thus the prince of the Most High, his messenger of salvation, will have every thing levelled before him, to effect the gathering of Israel and the establishment of the worship of the Lord, as it has been predicted by the prophets. And in all our sorrows, amidst all our wanderings, whenever we were banished from the places of our sojourning, we had before us this hope of a glorious deliverance, and of a messenger of redemption; and we were enabled to endure persecutions, bid defiance to inappeasable tyranny; and it was thus that our religion survived in our hearts, because we felt assured that it would at last reign triumphant, when the appointed time for the close of our sorrows, the end of the expiation of our iniquity, had come.

But there have arisen among us men who desire not to see their nation restored; who wish not to pray for the rebuilding of the temple; who ridicule the idea that again the sacrifice of Judah and Jerusalem will be pleasant to the Lord as in ancient days, and in years of antiquity; who profess to look for no greater happiness than to enjoy civil freedom in all the countries where we dwell; and who emphatically say that they do not believe in the personal Messiah, whom Israelites of former ages so ardently hoped for. And one of them has said that it is necessary to root out this belief from the hearts of Israelites, that they may not be seduced to believe in *Yisha' Notzri.* Hear it, brethren, we must destroy our faith, that we may not be induced to adopt a creed hateful to our souls! Was it for this that we endured so many martyrdoms, that we poured forth our blood in streams, testifying that we would believe only in one God, in no associate, in none besides our Father in heaven? Could Israel be ever seduced to adopt so false a conception of God, because they believe in a messenger whom He has promised? We reject the aspersion with scorn and contempt; we will remain faithful, and still trust in God's promises; we will not reject his glorious prediction out of fear that we might deny his being. We have been tried long and severely; and it is not for such an end that we have struggled, that we should adopt a creed which we have rejected times without number, when our death was demanded as the forfeit of our refusal.

I could spend several hours in reciting to you a

succession of prophecies from Moses to Malachi, to prove that a bodily Messiah has been predicted, and that the Scriptures cannot be fulfilled in any other manner, except by such an agent. But it is not necessary that I should do so; and I will merely extract one more passage, which will be enough to bring conviction home to any one who has confidence in the word of God. It is the conclusion of the fifty-ninth chapter of Isaiah: "And the redeemer shall come to Zion, and to those who return from transgression in Jacob. And as for myself, this is my covenant with them, saith the Lord, my spirit which is upon thee, and my word which I have put in thy mouth, shall not depart from thy mouth, and from the mouth of thy children, and the mouth of thy children's children, saith the Lord, from now unto eternity." You will see from the connexion of the ideas, that as little as the word of God shall depart from us, so shall the messenger of God, the Goël who is to effect his will, not remain absent when the transgressors in Jacob return to righteousness. There is no doubt expressed of this regeneration in spirit, no more than this has been done by Moses; it is certain, it is in the nature of things, it is the character of our people, and therefore did God select us from all other nations to receive his law, knowing as He did that, however rebellious and stubborn, we would never reject as a people the treasure He had given us. When, therefore, righteousness shall again have become the character of Jacob's sons, the redeemer, who is to release them from bondage to the laws not acknowledged by the divine code, shall appear, and restore the temple, and the sacrifices, and the priests, and the judges, and the people likewise, as they were aforetimes. But, say modern unbelievers, "we want none of these things; we are satisfied with freedom wherever we live; we do not require sacrifices, we do not desire a Palestine, we look for no prince, we would not obey him if he were here now, we are ardently attached to the republic here, as to the royalty there;" in brief, such men as these will not hope, will not pray for a redemption, they believe not in the future son of David who is to come, and some of these men endeavour to taint others with their unbelief, and to propagate through writing and speech their doctrines, which are opposed to the letter and spirit of God's word which is to live forever. Now, first as regards themselves, the prophet Ezekiel already spoke of such as these when he said: "And I will select out from you those who rebel and (wilfully) transgress against me; from the land of their sojourning will I bring them out, but to the land of Israel shall they not come, and you shall know that I am the Lord." What they despise will not be given them, and they will be deprived also of what they so ardently cling to. We may well leave their punishment in the hands of Him whose word will stand forever, as He will prove on them likewise that He is the Lord. But as respects their ridicule of our hopes, and their question how it is to be accomplished, we would remark, that had any one predicted in Egypt one hundred years before the birth of Moses, that a child should be born to a Hebrew mother, who would be educated by a daughter of Pharaoh as a prince in the royal palace, that this child, after learning all the wisdom of the priests and necromancers of that country, would at length return after a banishment of many years, require of the king the release of the Israelitish bondmen, and would, in consequence of this demand, work miracles, overthrow the idols of Egypt, effect the dismissal which he had asked, and become finally the means of promulgating an imperishable legislation : he would have unquestionably been looked upon as an idle dreamer, and been ridiculed for his insane ravings. Nevertheless, all this took place, and Moses, though educated in the palace of Pharaoh, never forgot his brothers who groaned under their burdens; he forfeited his life to the laws of Egypt in the moment of uncontrollable indignation, when he struck a taskmaster who was beating an Israelite, one of his own nation; he came back, and, in the name of the eternal God, did not beg for, but required the dismissal of a slave-nation that built the towns and magazines of the mighty king; he proved his right to be heard by signs and wonders, which overcame at length the tyrant's stubborn will; the idols of the people and the priests that served them were humbled before the prophet of the *new* God, new to that age though the Creator of the world; and at the foot of Sinai the redeemed heard the voice of the living God, and they received through Moses the details of the law which has survived to this day, and which from mere analogy we would be compelled to judge would outlast every new or contemporaneous idea, as it has done everything brought in competition with it hitherto. And after witnessing all this great display of divine power in a manner so remarkable and striking, shall we doubt that God can gather us again, and restore our nation and our worship? Only see, we then were slaves, ignorant, and sunk into the depths of pollution, as it has been allegorically said, that there are fifty gates of uncleanness, and the Israelites in Egypt had entered into all but one, and were thus well-nigh lost forever. And against this awful picture compare us as we are now; we have indeed sinned deeply; but for all this the law of God is with us, and we are in almost every land more or less adherents of its precepts; we are not sunk into the debasement of absolute slavery; we have a share in the progress of science and refinement: and can it be possible that we should declare in our unbelief, that the Lord cannot accomplish all his word which He has spoken?

Moreover, the progress of science is such at this day, that it is scarcely possible to say what can be accomplished through means of natural causes, which operate in a manner which would have been deemed fabulous not a century ago. The exhibition of the natural miracles of electricity, photography, and illumination by gas and similar things would, in the beginning of the last century, have exposed the possessor of these secrets of nature to the danger of being punished as a wizard. Yet now every one acknowledges them to be as they are, within the range of natural causes, and they are used daily without exciting more than ordinary attention. How shall we then determine now what can or cannot be and take place hereafter? We are met with the objection that at present the land of Israel is not fit for our occupation; it has become barren and parched, as though sulphur and salt had destroyed the soil: yes, it is so indeed; but the Hand that destroyed can also revive; the mountains can be again clad with verdure, and the valleys may again be hid under the weight of luxuriant crops. Now, and for centuries, the rains of heaven have been scarce, as they come down at uncertain periods. Suppose, then, that the first and the latter rains were to be sent again as in former ages, that the pools were to be filled with the refreshing element, the brooks blessed with a perennial flow, the wells again send forth water in abundance: would not the land be soon once more what it was,—fertile, beautiful, lovely, desirable? Now commerce is banished, because there is nothing for it to carry away. But suppose that the trade of the Eastern world were to seek once more its way across the newly restored land, to convey the products of the East to the land of the setting of the sun, and its goods, to where the sun rises out of the sea: would not the land of Israel be the home of universal commerce, the seat of power and refinement? Understand, all this can occur without calling into aid the power of miracles, or the change of a solitary law of nature: and shall we doubt, then, that the Lord can accomplish the promises He made to us through his prophets? We have so often tasted his bounty, been so often shielded by his mercy, that we would be ungrateful indeed, were mere incredulity to incline us to doubt of the good which is impending over us. The evil has come, we have received the punishment for our sins: the consolation, too, will, therefore, not be denied, the moment the time for its accomplishment shall have come.

But we shall be told, that we need not any greater blessing than the enjoyment of freedom; in this country we can work out the development of the divine idea, and prepare mankind for the acceptance of the truth, without desiring a separate national existence. O the blindness of unbelief! What have we here to boast of so greatly! You are at liberty, indeed, in Louisville and Cincinnati to carry on whatever business you please; you can keep a clothing-store or peddle about the country with a jewelry-box. But what are the beneficial results for the religion you profess? Is not a violation of its principles constantly excused on the plea, that it is impossible to be a strict Jew against the spirit and letter of the laws of the country? And suppose it were even otherwise, that you were subjected to no disqualification as Jews, which you decidedly are, when compared with other citizens: still it might be justly asked, Is this the proper pursuit for high-minded Israelites, to keep a clothing-store or deal in baubles and jewelry? Is there nothing nobler, nothing more fitting for the high intellect with which we are endowed, than to be the shopkeepers of the world? And still, while we are scattered everywhere, subjected to the laws of every state, and looked upon with suspicion and distrust by our fellow-citizens or fellow-subjects of other persuasions, we shall be compelled to exhibit, as a mass, the evidences of an inferiority which would be foreign to us, were we again a nation, a unit, a people having a government and a home of our own,— where we would be subject to no potentate, to no laws, save those of the great King, the holy One of Israel, our God, whose yoke עול מלכות שמים is no burden, but an ornament, a glorious distinction to him who wears it, which galls not the neck, which wounds not the shoulders, but brings healing and joy; where we should be ruled by a prince not governing by arbitrary enactments, and the mad fancies of an excited legislature, but leading all gently on the path of rectitude, as ordained by the divine precepts, protecting alike the great in their possessions, and shielding the humble against the assaults of those too mighty for them. What objection can any Israelite frame against such a government, where justice and freedom combined keep watch over the rights of all? Yes, let us then hope for and desire the advent of the sprout from the root of Jessé, under whom the outcasts of Israel will be gathered from the four corners of the earth, in the land which was given to our father Abraham.

Let us in the meanwhile, however, not be disheartened by the humble position which we occupy in the world, nor by the disregard which our religion meets with from the majority of mankind. For it was the word of God, which in olden days Isaiah was ordered to proclaim, that all is perishable save itself alone. Do not fret, therefore, that you are few, while the nations are many; because the promise of the Lord is with you to save and shield you. Do not be dismayed that the churches of the various sects are spread over the land as the grass of the field, while their towers reach heavenward as the flowers which rise above the grass. For there is a change impending, be it far away or hastening speedily, when all the external glory of the gentile-creeds will vanish, when the Lord will alone reign supreme over all; then will the churches, mosques, and temples vanish, because the wind of God will have blown upon them; then will the towers, and steeples, and monuments crumble into dust before the blast of the Most High which will pass over them, and all will dry up like the grass and wither like the flowers of the field; but the truth which is ours will then pervade all, and whoever has a spirit will worship God alone, at the time when He will send his messenger to redeem those who have waited for his salvation. And may He give to you all "glory instead of ashes, the oil of gladness instead of mourning, the mantle of glory instead of a grieved spirit," in the consolation of Jerusalem, in the rebuilding of the temple, in the restoration of the worship, in the reign of the son of David. Amen.

[NOTE. The above is the substance of a sermon delivered on Sabbath Nachamu, the 2d of August, 5617, at the Walnut Street Synagogue, Cincinnati.]

DISCOURSE VIII.

THE HOUSE OF THE TRUE GOD.*

BROTHERS OF THE HOUSE OF ISRAEL!

We have assembled to-day for the first time in this house, to dedicate it to the worship of the True God,

---

* In the spring of 5617 the new congregation, Beth El Emeth, "the House of the True God," was formed in Philadelphia, and I was elected Hazan and Preacher, on the 11th of Nissan. Immediate arrangements were made to acquire a synagogue, and, till it was finally opened on the 14th of Elul (3d of September), the new body never assembled, as such, for public worship. The opening sermon was intended to give the reasons for forming the Kahal, its sole object being to unite for the promotion of religion, and to cultivate good feeling with all Israelites. This idea has been carefully kept in view, and the result obtained has justified the movement, which many looked on at first with jealousy and suspicion.

to Him who created the heavens and the earth and all that fills universal space; and we accordingly devote it, during the time we or other Israelites have possession of this building, to the service of the Most High, in order that his Name may be invoked by all who may desire to associate with us in the adoration of the Being whose providence cares for all, and whose omniscience surveys all the secrets of the hearts of men.

We stand thus for the first time in the presence of our Maker as a new association of his adorers, with our wives and little ones, to declare that we also desire to be known as a special society among other communities of Israel, as men devoted to that cause which was handed down from the most ancient days as an heirloom of the descendants of Abraham; and that we are ready to labour with a thorough goodwill, with united hearts and souls, for the maintenance of the blessed faith which has been our life and preservation, even from the day that it was intrusted to our safe-keeping, when we were assembled at the foot of Horeb, until this hour when we are congregated in this house, which we have called that of the True God, of Him who was, who is, and who will be. It is, therefore, a momentous occasion which has called us together, and it well deserves to be pondered on, that it may never depart from our memory, while the spirit within us is united to the perishable frame, while the divine spark which constitutes our life is connected with the mortal clay which is its dwelling, and that the recollection may accompany us to the moment when the angel of death comes to release the soul, to bear it away to its resting-place at the foot of Mercy's throne.—Let us take for our text, Joshua xxii. 34:

ויקראו בני ראובן ובני גד למזבח כי עד הוא בינתינו
כי ה' האלהים:

"And the children of Reuben and the children of Gad called the altar (*Ed*); for (they said), It is a witness between us that the Eternal One is God."

This passage occurs in one of the last chapters of the book of Joshua, and is the conclusion of the history of the altar which the two and half tribes, whose domain was on the east side of the Jordan, had erected on the bank of that river, when they returned to their homes, after having assisted the western tribes in conquering the land of Canaan. It is well known to you, that no altar was permitted to be erected in the whole country of Israel besides the one which was near the tabernacle, and later, the temple on Moriah. When, therefore, news was brought to the other Israelites of this occurrence, they at once assembled at Shiloh to send out an army against what they thought the rebellious tribes, to coerce them to obedience. But before proceeding to such extremes they despatched a deputation of eleven of the principal chiefs, among whom was the zealous Phineas, prudent as he was daring, to remonstrate with the men of Reuben and their confederates on account of the great transgression of which they presumed them guilty. These, however, answered deprecatingly, and said, "The God of gods, the Eternal One, the God of gods, the Eternal One, He knoweth, and Israel also shall know: if it be in rebellion, or if in transgression against the

Lord (aid us not this day), that we have built us an altar to turn away from following the Lord; or if to offer thereon burnt-offering, or meat-offering, or if to offer thereon peace-offerings, may the Lord himself require it." In the same strain they continued to asseverate their good intentions, and finished by saying that it should be regarded as a perpetual testimony between the portions of Israelites divided from each other by the Jordan, that both the ones and the others believed in the same God, whom they all then adored. And when Phineas and his companions had been gratified by this declaration of faith, and had departed for their homes, the trans-Jordanic tribes gave to the altar the name which designated it to be to them a testimony, that in every possible contingency of life the Lord should be alone their God, and that they would regard his altar at the tabernacle as the only centre of worship,—thus pledging themselves to offer up their devotions solely after the manner laid down in the divine law. It is well to understand distinctly the condition of the world when the Reubenites and their immediate confederates made this avowal: The legislation of Sinai was yet new, and they were only the second generation that had become familiar with it; all around them, nay, in their own country and neighbourhood, were many tribes that worshipped idols, indulged in carnal practices interdicted by the Mosaic law, and, in brief, were as different in thought and action from the standard of righteousness which they had themselves received, as it is possible to be. They were, therefore, exposed through many temptations to fall off by degrees from the road of life they had travelled under Moses and Joshua, and to become either like the Egyptians, in whose land they had been bondmen, or like the Canaanites, among whom they then dwelt. It was no doubt this consideration which impelled the assembled Israelites at Shiloh to endeavour to crush what they supposed the incipient infection of pagan life, by a terrible blow, though a universal carnage of the rebels might be the result. But the suspected tribes, on the contrary, then declared that they did not desire to multiply places of sacrifice, after the manner of the idolaters, who fancied that frequent acts of devotion, performed in many places, were requisite to propitiate their gods; but that they would, after the simpler fashion of the Scripture-commands, resort only to the spot chosen by God out of all their tribes, to offer up there, and there alone, all that had been commanded, and just as it had been ordained; and that the very altar they had erected on the banks of the Jordan, standing, as it should, in solitude and silence, without smoke to arise from its hearth, without a priest to keep watch near it, without the festive crowd to encamp in its precincts on the stated seasons of pilgrimage, should prove in the strongest manner that the structure was merely a testimony to all beholders that the stream which divides Palestine into two unequal parts, did not separate the people into two sects; but that both the inhabitants of the East and the West were bound together by the ties of one faith, having one country, one origin, one religion, one altar, and one God!

We, too, my friends, stand here this day before the world with a new structure which we have dedicated to the cause of religion; but it is not a new faith which is to be symbolized here, no new worship which is to be introduced within these walls; and all Israel, if all were witnesses here this day, should see, that neither in rebellion, nor in transgression against the Most High, nor in malevolence towards our brothers of other societies, has the work been begun and thus far completed; but to cement the stronger our adherence to God's most holy law, and to fortify ourselves in the attachment to the whole household of Israel, which was once so strong and beautiful, but which has, alas! so greatly waned in the troublous times through which we have had to pass. You must not forget, my brothers, that, though we are not surrounded by the idols of Egypt, nor by the abominations of Canaan, our warfare with the world without is not accomplished. Our faith has its enemies in the circumstance that we are still a peculiar people, with laws which separate us from the board and communion of non-Israelites; in the fact that we adore a NAME who is not yet enthroned alone and solely in the hearts of man, though He is alone and solely the TRUE GOD, the Creator of all things. Political power and influence are, as such, no necessary appendage to the household of Israel; but we are scattered, strewn like the seed from the pouch of the ploughman, over the surface of the earth, to be controlled and trammelled by all who differ from us, and who unite in this, when even differing ever so widely among themselves, that it is for the benefit of the world at large, that the Hebrew race should be watched and kept within the narrowest possible bounds, lest their creed should spread, and their religion attain to that degree of power, that it might work an injury unto those modes of thought and practice to which the various sections of mankind are devoted. This hostility is at the same time not always a mere passive dislike, which shows itself in an unwillingness to associate with us on terms of equality, and to grant us that weight in the historical development of the world which would of right be due to our industry, probity, and intelligence, or in short, to treat us as one man usually treats the other; but in many quarters of the globe active measures of repression and coercion are resorted to, in order to vex us with restraints and burdens from which others are exempt, and to offer all possible inducements to those, whose heart is not sincere, to forsake a faith which brings no worldly gain, and to cast off the connexion with a people, which the laws of the land and public prejudice stigmatize as inferior to the other classes of the inhabitants. Though millions of martyrs have at all periods of history testified by their death, under incredible tortures of body and mind, that no suffering was capable to withdraw them from their God and his law: still experience has proved that many have yielded to the allurement of public offices to either become apostates altogether, or to shape their conduct so that their Judaism was rendered undistinguishable to the unpractised eye, so that such as these at times boast of having so well disguised their inherited religion, as not to be suspected of belonging to its adherents. Others again there are who daily make the amount of duties to be performed less and less; because they fancy themselves exempt from its behests in this enlightened age of the world, and so approximate the gentile freedom from the precepts, that they gradually lapse into infidelity, or they unconsciously almost, join one of the sects around them, and this perhaps, not immediately in their own persons, but in those of their offspring, who, never having been initiated into the practice of the duties of Judaism, and never having been imbued with the full force and beauty of the doctrines which lie as the basis of our lives, have no safeguard to ward off temptation, nor any tangible reasons for remaining nominally Jews when all the substance has long since been evaporated into air in the life of their progenitors, by a constantly more accelerated process of spiritualizing those distinctive acts which, by the scriptural enactments, ought to distinguish the conduct of every son of Israel. This latter species of apostacy is more common where we enjoy a moderate or entire share of equality of civil and political rights, than where we are oppressed and excluded from participating in the privileges of citizenship. The very distance of the danger will bring us within its grasp. Tell a man, when he begins to acquire wealth and distinction, that he has taken the first step to banish his sons from the precincts of the synagogue, and he will exhibit all the appearances of offended rectitude. For he will tell you, that he is engaged in a pursuit which will exhibit him to the world as an ornament to human nature; that he trusts, with the help of Heaven, to prove what the Jew is capable of achieving if his genius is unchecked; and that he will nevertheless take heed that all in his household shall know that they are Israelites, the possessors of a faith of which they should justly be proud. But if we look on him again at a later period, we may find that he has by degrees relaxed the strict discipline which once prevailed in his home; that he has so many engagements, that he is not able to watch all the walks in which his children tread the course of life; that while he toils for large gains, or fame and position, they seek each their own pleasures; become more and more strangers to the house of God; lapse by degrees into non-Jewish society; form intimacies which deaden the last spark of devotion in their souls; and that they succeed, perchance, to withdraw their aged and now helpless parents from the close communion with their brothers, ashamed and degraded in their own estimation, or entrapped into actual transgression, by the misconduct of those who, they once vainly hoped, would perpetuate their name as a house honoured among the descendants of Jacob. By this process of self-exaltation, and a gradually increasing contempt for the association with other Israelites, which led the children to cast off the little restraint the parental teaching had at first imposed on them, families once numerous among us are approaching their extinction, and it is possible that in a few generations not one of them will be left to swear fealty to the Eternal God. Yet the transition was very slow at first; in the beginning it was perhaps a substitution of the first for the seventh day of the week as the Sabbath of the Lord; next visiting places of instruction where a faith different from ours was taught; then a gradual withdrawal from those who were professing Jews, because they stood not as high in the world's estimation; then the covenant of Abraham was neglected; or the daughter or the son of the stranger entered into family-relations with the child of Jacob: and thus the way was left open for a quiet mingling as a member with one of the non-Jewish associations; and in this way a name and a family have perished in Israel.

But not alone those in an exalted position are thus lost to us; many in inferior positions imitate the evil example set them by the others; and they mingle with the debauchee and the outcast, there to indulge their wicked inclinations, forsaking thereby the home where humble piety dwells, and departing from the path of the law, to their entire ruin. It is not necessary to produce illustrations from our experience to prove the truth of what I have just uttered; for all of you may, if they will tax their memory, verify my words by what has fallen under their own observation; and they will therefore acknowledge that we are not exempt from danger in the present posture of events, though we live not in the midst of idolaters, as did the Reubenites when they built the altar near the Jordan. Let us, therefore, avail ourselves of this occasion to reflect on the work before us. We enter this day into a covenant with God, tacitly, if not in words, to be faithful to Him, and to preserve the law "which is an inheritance of the congregation of Jacob" for those who are to come after us. We bind ourselves, by devoting this house especially to the attribute of "Truth," which is the seal of the Creator under which He called the world into being, that we will guard the faith with all our strength against the encroachment of error from whatever side this might threaten it, and to show ourselves truthful in a singleness of devotion to the precepts we have received. We shall be indeed approached with appeals as to the unreasonableness of an adherence to antiquated notions and practices; but this is the very purpose which ought to engage us; and to succeed we ought to search into what has come down from the days of antiquity. Our very name is as ancient as history. Abraham was surnamed the *Hebrew*, and this designation yet denotes his descendants; Jacob was blest and called Israel, and we are therefore the proper Israelites of whose future so much is said in the Holy Scriptures, and of whom so many hopeful anticipations are entertained. It would be now insulting to sound human reason to pause here to prove that it would be impossible to preserve the identity of the Israelites without the bond of the law; as, without this, they would soon cease to be distinguishable among the rest of mankind, and would thus disappear as agents from the work of history. But to check the deterioration which was just alluded to, and to preserve the identity of our race, which many have lost already, we ought to resort to those measures which were found so efficacious in the days of Hezekiah and Josiah, kings of Judah, and of Ezra and Nehemiah, when the Babylonian captivity had been terminated by the rebuilding of the temple of Jerusalem. These means were, first, a greater cordiality among the people, a more intimate union for the purpose of furthering the observance of the precepts of the Scriptures, and, secondly, an earnest endeavour to render all more familiar with the contents of the Scriptures than they had been before. At a future day we shall no doubt recur to this topic at greater length; our present purpose is merely to sketch an outline of what is needed. When we were still under one government, and had a country which we could call our own, the heads of the state, such as judges, kings, princes, governors, and high-priests, could, by their political power and influence, contribute largely to the direct improvement of religion and morals; hence we find that, in proportion as our rulers were virtuous and pious, the people were so likewise. But at present, other influences must be brought to bear on us, and they are, simply, association and individual exertions. As regards the first, let us observe that no matter how great a mind may dwell in any man, he cannot labour except in a very limited sphere; he can be only in one place at a time, and he is therefore liable to be counteracted and defeated by the next comer, not so much by the superior power of the other, as by his own absence, through which means his influence is overcome by, perhaps, the mere assurance and impudent, bold, assertions of the other. It is for this reason nothing new, that public bodies exhibit the inconstancy of the sea, as they are swayed often, not by a positive rule of right, but by the opinion of the latest teacher. To avoid this uncertainty and constant fluctuation, it is necessary to associate together on a basis of unvarying principles, and to establish a rule which nothing shall be able to overthrow. You have attempted to carry this into practice, my friends, in the constitution you have adopted, by laying down the irrevocable rule that you will, as a body, have only those prayers which the great lights of Israel delighted to employ in their addressing Him "who sitteth on the throne of mercy;" and in so doing, you also declare that you will faithfully and truly abide by the principles which the words of these prayers inculcate.* You have farther declared that only Israelites in practice shall have a controlling power in your assemblies; the doors of this house shall indeed stand open wide, to admit every one, the righteous one and the sinner, the son of Abraham and him whose parentage is not of Israel, to offer up here their devotion, and to pour out their heart before the Lord in joy or in sorrow; since God himself has taught us that his house should be a house of prayer to all people. At the same time it has been resolved on wisely, to exclude all from the control of affairs whose own conduct would stamp them as unfit to be trusted with a voice in the religious concerns of Israel. Having thus commenced, let us hope that you will feel the weight of the obligation resting on you, and that you will resolve to leave nothing untried to induce each other to be strict in the observance of all those duties in which so many are deficient, especially the keeping of the Lord's Sabbath, that this house may not be empty, while those, who have an interest here, seek their worldly gains in their places of business; we will trust that you will stimulate each other to give all the children a knowledge of their faith and of the language of Israel, that, when they come hither, the words of the prayers may be familiar to their ears, and not sound to them like an unmeaning jargon

---

* This alludes to the clause in the constitution which requires a unanimous vote for a change in the form of worship, based on the so-called Portuguese Prayer-book as printed in Amsterdam. None but those married according to the Jewish Laws, and circumcising their children, can be members of the congregation, while *all* may come and worship without distinction as to religion or their delinquency.

which makes nothing but an unpleasant impression on the mind. But individual exertions must not be omitted, nor should any one wait to move in the expectation that the public will and ought to go first forward. Whatever strikes either of you as useful and practicable, he ought to bring before the community and request in a courteous manner their co-operation; and in case it does not meet with as prompt support as he has perhaps a right to expect, he should endeavour to see what he can do alone, and labour to awake public attention to his plan, and in the meanwhile accomplish all that an individual, single-handed, is able to attain. Persuasion, honesty of purpose, and unflagging industry, are almost unfailing means in insuring success; and the empire of religion also needs servants animated with these qualities to achieve a triumph over the enemies that oppose its progress.

This is our object and purpose, *union for the sake of our ancient faith*, and for this each individual, let us hope, will labour with all his soul; and as far as the efforts of him, whom you have chosen as the *messenger* of your congregation, can avail, he pledges himself, that whatever gifts of mind the Most Gracious One has endowed him with, shall be devoted to the same end, so that through us the name of God may be glorified in some little measure. Much, feeble man cannot promise; he can accomplish but little; it is only in the hands of the Almighty to bestow success on all enterprises. This, however, we can safely declare, that it is not in rebellion against the Lord, nor to turn away from Him, that we have established this house of prayer, nor from motives of malevolence against our brothers, that we meet here to perform our devotions: towards the Lord we declare, that we will abide by the faith as our fathers delivered it to us; and to our brothers we hold out the hand of fellowship, and we pledge ourselves that we will, if in our power, act with all of them in unison to forward all measures tending to the public welfare; and while we invoke the blessing of God on our enterprise, we also crave the good-will of all Israelites towards ourselves and this house, in which we shall hereafter assemble. And we farther declare, that this house, and any other which may in future be built, in case it should happen that the space here be not large enough to receive all the worshippers that may resort hither to unite with us in the adoration of the Most High, shall be forever a witness against us in the judgment of God, that we mean now and for all time, as a congregation of Israelites, to believe firmly and faithfully in the sole existence of the Eternal God, who alone created the heavens and formed the earth, whose spirit gives knowledge, whose mercy saves, and whose power delivers; yes, that we will be servants in life and unto death of the Omnipotent One, who delivered our fathers from Egypt, and who will gather their descendants unto his holy mountain, under the guidance of his anointed, the son of David. Amen.

O Father and King! God of Abraham, Isaac, and Israel, look down from thy high and holy dwelling on the children of the dust, who have essayed to devote to Thee another house, where thy Name may abide among the descendants of thy servants. We know our weakness, and that we are dust,—here this day in health and prosperity, soon to be laid in the grave, to moulder away as our fathers before us. Only Thou livest to eternity, and to thy days there is no ending. We therefore turn to Thee, to crave thy presence with us in our coming on, that much spiritual blessing may flow unto us from the meetings within these walls, so that the taught and the teachers may issue thence invigorated by thy consolation, and instructed in the knowledge of thy ways. Let us also be strengthened by thy inspiration, that the words of thy law may be pleasant to us, so that they may fructify within us, and render us obedient to thy behests, and willing to follow Thee, O Father! whether we live in prosperity, or perish in earthly misery. Let thy wisdom animate us, that we may be shown how to distinguish between the true and the false, between the apparent good and the real evil; that we may walk safely before Thee, and not be ensnared by the power of sin.

Let the spirit of counsel and understanding rest on the managers of this congregation and its members, that they may resolve only on what will tend to promote thy kingdom and spread good-will and friendship among all thy servants who dwell in this city. And wherever thy children dwell, let them be made conscious that they are thine, whom Thou didst purchase as thy servants, when Thou didst redeem them from Egyptian slavery, that they might proclaim thy glory and spread thy Name unto all the corners of the earth.—On the rulers and people of this city and country also display thy grace, that peace may dwell here, and the clashing of armour not be heard, and plenty and contentment reign everywhere around us;

so that we of thy household, whose lot is cast here, may not be disturbed by the sound of battles, nor the pinching of famine, nor by political violence or oppression, and thus prevented from pursuing the course marked out to us in thy law, which is the life and permanence of Israel. Yea, be with us all in our comings in and goings out, and let us feel thy presence wherever we may be assembled; and give us the strength to proclaim thy glory and to propagate thy faith; and let us be made conscious that Thou art indeed our God, even the Creator of the world, the God of Truth, to all eternity. Amen.

DISCOURSE IX.

THE ISRAELITES' THANKSGIVING.*

My Friends!

We are assembled here this day in accordance with the recommendation of the Governor of this commonwealth, who, in conjunction with the chief magistrates of other states, has set it apart as a day of thanking the Most High for the many benefits which He has bestowed on this land, and to invoke the continuance of his kindness. Although we Israelites have done this already on our own festivals which we lately celebrated, especially on the Day of Atone-

---

* Address delivered on the 29th of November, 5621, at the Franklin Street synagogue, Philadelphia.

ment, when we prayed for peace and for abundance during the coming year, and the Feast of Tabernacles, when we returned thanks for the gifts which the past season had brought us: we still unite ourselves this day with our fellow-citizens of other persuasions to repair to the houses of our God, to offer up to Him the grateful offering of our thankful hearts. For, as we are the political equals with men of all creeds, we must not be absent in any matter in which we have all a common interest, although our religion makes it our duty to observe certain periods as especially devoted to the exercise of that obligation, which the executives of various states in this country request the citizens at large to offer, as a voluntary acknowledgment of their indebtedness at the close of the harvest, when the abundant increase of the field has blessed the labour of the husbandman.

The question then arises: "How shall we be thankful?" Is it enough that we resort to the places of devotion, and recite there, from burning lips, a multitude of words which convey the expressions of gratitude? This would evidently not be enough; for how often do the most fervent words leave the heart cold and unimpressed; and even while a man in so many words acknowledges his dependence on divine bounty, he may in his own heart ascribe his success to his own skill, and his escape from evil to his own prudence.—How, then, shall we thank God? To solve this question let us refer to the teaching of our prophets, from whom we have in all cases ample directions for our conduct. When a portion of the people of Judah had been carried away as captives to Babylon, at the time when the rest of our state was

THE ISRAELITES' THANKSGIVING. 151

hastening to decay, Jeremiah sent to those exiled already a message to the effect that they should take an interest in their new home, and then added:

ודרשו את שלום העיר אשר הגליתי אתכם שמה
והתפללו בעדה אל ה' כי בשלומה יהיה לכם שלום:

"And seek ye the welfare of the city whither I have banished you, and pray in its behalf unto the Lord; for in its welfare shall ye fare well," or literally, in the Hebrew idiom, "in its peace shall ye have peace." Jeremiah xxix. 7.

It is thus made the duty of the Israelite to identify himself with the country in which he resides, contribute to its prosperity, and invoke Heaven's blessing for its welfare, and, in fulfilment of these duties, he will best show himself grateful for the common blessings which he enjoys as a citizen, and the peculiar privilege of being a son of Israel. Let us, then, trace the line of conduct he ought to pursue.

This age is emphatically one of self-sufficiency. Whatever is old meets with but little consideration, and the wisdom of past ages is held in light esteem by those who now play their part on the earth. This has produced its mischievous influence on our religious conformity; since it is well known to you, how little we represent in our conduct the practices of our fathers. What they deemed as sacred is not regarded by many of us as such, and defection meets us wherever we turn our view. But the same is the case in the political world. A constitution which was framed scarcely more than seventy years ago, and was then justly esteemed as the perfection of human wisdom, has already lost much of its power in a land which it was calculated to bless, and men who love change and excitement have, by their unwise agitation, brought this confederacy to the brink of dissolution; and in this land where men fondly hoped that human freedom might be firmly established for many centuries, undisturbed by war's alarms, we hear the rumbling of the distant thunder of tumult and strife spreading over once peaceful plains and securely sheltered valleys.* Why is this? Because it is as though a skilfully constructed machine had been placed in charge of an inexperienced boy, who is totally ignorant of the levers, valves, pistons, and wheels which are necessary for its government and safety, and forces, in his ignorance, a stake or spike where it ought not to be, in order to improve it, and thereby causes an explosion, which destroys the elegant fabric and himself likewise. It is the presumption, then, of those who are not satisfied with the amount of good they themselves enjoy, and thoughtlessly intermeddle with the rights of others, which cannot, after all, injure them in any manner; and this produces, accordingly, as its natural effects, the heartburning and strife which are manifest to all, and the danger which even now threatens this land, so much favoured in the fertility of the soil and the freedom of its institutions.

Imagine not, however, my friends, that I am going to make a political speech; for this is not the place where it should be delivered, nor do I think it my province to venture on the task.—But we have a common interest in the state, and are commanded to

---

* This was spoken just before the breaking out of the late civil war in the United States.

labour and pray for its welfare; and, therefore, we have also to see to it, that we avoid contributing, by any act of ours, to injure the peace of the country where we are so pre-eminently blessed in the possession of freedom. As citizens, we should accordingly eschew all connexion with agitators, who, from ignorance or selfishness, might work injury to the commonwealth. It is true, our numbers are but small; we can, therefore, exert but little influence on public affairs, and our weight can scarcely be felt. But, for all this, we should strive to show by our whole conduct, that we are fully alive to our duties, and that we are willing to discharge all the obligations which can be expected of us. We should be distinguished for good citizenship, so that, though few, we may be known as those who contribute, for their numbers, their full share to the welfare and peace of the state.

We should, therefore, avoid ever being counted among those who urge others to extremes. When parties differ on any point of policy, and they stand opposed to each other in an uncompromising attitude, and neither yields any of its pretensions, and both irritate each other by taunts and bitter speech: the peace of a country can soon be destroyed, and the work of master-minds be overthrown by the most ignorant, just as the boy in charge of a machine, to which I just alluded, can readily break into pieces in a moment what has cost months of skill and labour to produce. Be you, therefore, peacemakers; endeavour to soothe, wherever you can, the feelings of irritation, and do not contribute, by your acts or words, to increase the dangers which may threaten the state at any time. Serve the country faithfully; but to do so you need not be noisy in your demonstration, and by that means help to fan the flame of discord, if it ever be kindled. But you should quietly fulfil your duties; and, above all, be true to the commonwealth in which you live, and so demean yourselves, that the name of Israel shall suffer no damage at your hands, and be assured that in this manner you will best discharge whatever you owe to your fellowmen in quality of citizens.

This line of conduct is the more obligatory on us, from the fact that the various states composing this Union are becoming more alive to the claim of Israelites to an absolute equality, and of our being duly recognized on all public occasions. It was not long since that, when some chief magistrates issued their proclamation for a thanksgiving, or public fast-day, they worded the same in such a manner that we felt ourselves naturally precluded from uniting with our fellow-citizens in their acts of devotion. But by a respectful insisting on our rights, and not by noisy demonstration, we have succeeded in this, that in the greater part of the states we are invited with all others, equally with all other denominations, to return our thanks, or to offer up our prayers to our common heavenly Benefactor, and this simple change is to us a great cause of additional thankfulness, and a real progress which God has obtained for us. It is, therefore, not too much for us to assert, that it is highly probable that after a while our conduct as citizens, provided it be all it should be, will not fail to have its good effects for the welfare of the state in which our lot is cast, and that the morality which distinguishes us as individuals may extend its beneficial influence on many beyond our own circle.

Let us now revert to the effect of modern self-sufficiency on our religious state, which affects us as Israelites particularly. It is, indeed, too lamentably true that many of us have learned to disregard all positive religious duties, and they have made themselves a new code of their own invention. They neglect the laws of the Most High, and listen to the voice of the passions, or their own private interests, and reject all which does not coincide with their fancy. But not alone is this evil to be observed among the common people; for among teachers likewise has the defection spread, and the divine law is viewed as something which has ceased to have any real value, which must yield to the wisdom of the present age. Nay, what is more, they treat it as already dead, they subject it to their vain criticism, and they submit it to their dissecting knife, presumptuously selecting from the dissevered limbs what they imagine suitable for their purpose, and then, by a process of galvanizing of their own, they endeavour to recall these fragments into life. I tell you nothing unknown to yourselves, my friends! it is evident to you all, and it is needless to hide the fact, that this present century has seen the power of God's word gradually losing its influence over the minds of Israelites, especially in this country of universal freedom, where it is our reproach that indifference to all that is sacred has reached its highest point. In many cases Hebrews seem ashamed of their faith, and they so carefully conceal the practices which their religion justly demands of them, that they are only glad when their origin as Jews escapes the knowledge of those among whom they mingle. But is it reasonable that in this country and in this land we should thus exhibit ourselves before the Benefactor of Israel? His revelation was to us a treasure in times of affliction, when we were persecuted everywhere; and to this day it has lost none of its sacredness and blissful efficacy, if we would only listen to the wisdom of the past, and follow the paths which our fathers have trod.

In times gone by it was not granted to us to live in peace, or to remain unharmed. The most absurd charges were invented against us, and for their sake we had to endure the greatest tortures. And then compare with these trials the present change which has been wrought for us: and I ask you, Have we not cause to thank our God for the mercy He has shown us in breaking our chains, and making us free? Imagine not, my friends, that it is merely the progress of civilization which has caused all this. For the change is too great to be merely human work. Compare our present position with that in the Middle Ages, when, for instance, the pestilence, known as the Black Death, swept over Europe, and carried off its millions of victims, and when, because comparatively few Israelites perished, it was charged against them that they had poisoned the sources of life, the springs and wells whence the water for drinking was obtained, in order to destroy the followers of Christianity. It was nothing to the brutalized multitudes that the charge could not be true, that many Jews, too, fell before the blows of the destroyer. And in all the towns along the Rhine, in Switzerland and Germany, the mob assailed our people, who in vain called for protection from the magistrates, and the only method they could find to escape from their lawless persecutors was to fall, uncontaminated, by their own hands, so that the best gift which they could bestow on their wives and children was to slay them themselves, before they fell into the hands of those who had neither mercy nor pity, and laughed with scorn over the misery of the helpless children of Israel. It was nothing rare then to see five hundred, a thousand, or two thousand Hebrews immolated in one day; and yet they clung to their faith, and went rejoicing to their end, since thus they could show their firm adherence to the Guardian of Israel.

Now, compare the state just merely sketched with our present position, where there is no distinction between us and our fellow-citizens, where we can assemble in our synagogues and examine, if we will, without hindrance or molestation, the religious systems or dogmas of those differing from us: and then say that we have not an especial cause of gratitude towards that Providence which has produced this wonderful change, even without reverting to the barbarities which were witnessed in Spain and Portugal, where the adherents of our faith were systematically hunted down, and tried as criminals for believing in the God of Israel. If even we concede much to the refinement produced by the spread of science, it is, after all, more owing to the greater diffusion of the Scriptures, which has humanized mankind, and broken the bonds of tyranny. Do we, therefore, do well, when, in the midst of freedom, we forget our Benefactor, and turn our back on the precepts which He has prescribed for us? I repeat, the distance between the Middle Ages and the present time is too great to be otherwise than an especial act of Providence; and, therefore, we ought to show by our conduct that we fully appreciate the mercy extended to us, by observing the precepts of that religion for which we then so greatly suffered, and which we can now so freely practise here, without fear of outward power being exerted to prevent our doing so, or punishing us for professing openly the principles which we hold sacred.

"And seek ye the welfare of the city whither I have banished you," are the words of the text. We can do this in the best manner by upholding the character of ancient Israel, its frugality, industry, and moral integrity. Republican governments find their safest support in the sturdy virtue of their inhabitants. No country can be free, or remain so long, where corruption and luxury are the rule, where sobriety and moderation are not dear to the citizens. Without referring to our own commonwealth, which perished when we had ceased to be deserving of independence, we may cite Greece and Rome, as also the Italian republics of the Middle Ages. The moment luxury prevailed; the moment that corruption infected those who were to administer the affairs of the state; the moment that women were but overdressed dolls; the moment that manly strength yielded to effeminacy,—that moment that usurpers from amidst the very people assumed the control of their debased countrymen, and the tottering fabrics became an easy prey to crafty and unscrupulous adventurers, who were able to gather around them those who were willing to aid their schemes, for a prospective reward from the destroyers of their country's liberty. No land can remain free where the citizens are no longer virtuous, where justice is disregarded, where industry is no longer honourable. When the public mind has become enslaved, the mere semblance of outward freedom is soon chased away; and first aristocracies and then tyrannies follow, in the natural course, to subject the many to their control. If, then, we indeed wish to seek the welfare of the land where we live, we must, as far as in us lies, uphold republican virtues, and thus contribute to the permanence of those franchises under the shadow of which we find peace.

But it must be evident to you, from what has been said already, that we cannot walk erect in the path of virtue, if we ascribe the success of the government to mere human wisdom; for it is this precisely which engenders pride, forgetfulness of duty, indulgence of the passions, and next, the downward course of degeneracy. No! all who wish truly to keep themselves and the state free from this calamity, should look on High for aid, and ascribe to the Almighty the glory due to his Name. In the words of the Psalmist, "Sing praises to God, sing praises; sing praises unto our King, sing praises." (Psalm xlvii. 7.) It is He that dispenses the sunshine, and sends the rain; it is He that endows the earth with fruitfulness, and blesses her increase. And it is He, too, by whose dispensation princes rule, and who gives stability to the counsels of men, provided they govern according to his spirit. Not, therefore, through unbelief, not by disdaining the instruction of God, not by departing from the road which our fathers have travelled, can we build up the welfare of this land, but by strictly adhering to all that our God has commanded us to do, and by asking Him for light on all our ways.

Yes, we should be grateful to God, and thank Him for all his mercies which He has bestowed on us so bountifully, without our contributing anything towards the change which has been wrought in our behalf. But, "with what shall we come before the Lord? bow ourselves before the God on high?" Shall we bring Him our children as sacrifices? or slaughter thousands of cattle? pour out rivers of oil and streams of wine on his altar? Shall mighty forests fall before our axe, that the wood thereof may be kindled into a vast fire, to consume the holocaust we thus bring to the Lord of all? Nothing of this is needed, brothers, sisters of Israel, youth and maidens of our race! but bring yourselves as the sacrifice, train yourselves to follow the divine commands on each and every day of your existence. There is something glorious in a consistent, pious course of life, which nothing on earth can excel in beauty. Picture before you a devoted servant of God practising deeds of righteousness from his first awakening to a sense of his responsibility, until he stands at length, with trembling steps, at the brink of the grave, with the consciousness of a well-spent life chasing away the gloom of death: and surely it is a boon worth living for, to possess the assurance that life has not been an idle indulgence in sensual pleasures, but has been devoted to the best interests of the soul and the happiness of mankind.

But I will not dwell any longer on this, what I might term a slight pen and ink sketch of a perfect character; a few bold outlines are enough to fix it on your attention, and to claim for it your admiration. If, however, you feel the necessity of acting yourselves as this example would naturally demand from you: let me entreat you to take heed that your children and charges shall not be less than you sincere adherents of your ancestral religion. And if you wish truly to labour for the welfare of the country, then endeavour to raise those who are to live after you in a manner that they may be able to withstand temptation, and not fall off on the path of transgression through your fault and example. Let them see you earnest in your piety, let them not detect duplicity in your conduct towards God; but teach them to be fully devoted to that faith which you ostensibly consider the best. Let them not, by your unwise indulgence, be permitted gradually to lapse into irreligion and immorality, and be you not the occasion that, when they leave your house to mingle with the world at large, they may sooner or later come back to your door beggars in pocket, with soiled hands and tattered garments, but, what is worse still, beggars in spirit, with trembling limbs, made prematurely old through the indulgence of their passions, by their partaking of those pleasures which destroy, before the natural time, the vigour of the human frame. For, dreadful as it would be to behold your offspring reduced to destitution through your neglect to train them properly, it would be frightful to be conscious that it was your own doing that they have become beggars in spirit, outcasts from their faith, which you failed to render dear to them. I will not detain you here likewise, but leave you to fill up the picture, satisfied that when you sincerely reflect, you cannot hesitate to take heed that your children and wards, those whom Providence has placed under your care, shall not have cause to accuse you hereafter that you led them astray from the path in which your example and influence might have kept them.

Let it be your endeavour, my friends, in accordance with what I have presented to you, to be proud of your religion when you mingle with the world. Let it be seen that you feel it a glory to belong to Israel, and wait not with your profession of faith till it be accidentally discovered. When the weekly Sabbath comes, consecrate it boldly to the service of your God: be not ashamed to abstain from your labour on that day, though all your neighbours pursue then their usual avocations. You owe this sacrifice to God, as an acknowledgment for the freedom with which He has blessed you here. When you sit among persons of a different belief, partake not of their viands from complacency or to hide your own convictions. Reflect, that it is not long since when to be an Israelite would have excluded you from such society, when you would have been avoided because of your origin. Give, therefore, thanks to your God, by mixing with men of other persuasions, without yielding in the least your duty from a mere complaisance to their prejudices; be firm, and sacrifice your appetite on the altar of your religion.

For only when you are consistent Israelites in your own persons, and when you train your children to continue worthily after your decease the noble race of the Patriarchs, can you be deserving of the many favours which you have received from the Lord. Then only can you properly fulfil the duties of citizenship which your country demands of you. For it is only the man who is fully imbued with the spirit of religion, who trusts in God, and believes himself safe with Him in life and death, that can sacrifice his property and, if need be, his blood and his earthly existence in the service of his country; and therefore *it* will have the best guarantee for your fidelity to it, in the adherence you show to your God and his *law*. And then, too, you have a right to pray to the Almighty for the welfare of the government, and for the peace of all the inhabitants who are sheltered under its protection, and then, also, you have reason to expect that the All-merciful, who watches all our deeds, will, in sending his blessing on the land where we sojourn, bestow on you also his peace and his bounty as a reward for your obedience to his will. Your thanksgiving, therefore, should not consist merely in words, be they ever so eloquent, nor in psalmody, be it ever so melodious, but in the sacrifice of yourselves, in the sacrifice of your inclinations, and in the rearing of your children to the service of the God of Israel: and thus only can you secure by your acts, and contribute by your words to the welfare of the land wherein you dwell.

DISCOURSE X.

ISRAEL AND CIVILIZATION.*

Brethren and Friends!

We are met here this afternoon to dedicate to the God of Israel this roomy structure which you have acquired as your house of prayer. The old building in which you have hitherto worshipped has become too small and too inconvenient for the numbers who seek it to unite in prayer to your God and Creator, and the large assembly now present testifies that you rejoice because the work you contemplated has been accomplished. But in this feeling of pious contentment, you must not forget for what purpose you dedicate, nor be unmindful of Him for whose glory you devote it. It is the Lord our God who is to be adored here, and it is his law which is to be taught here; and yet He is not alone your God, but the God of all the earth, the Sovereign of the whole universe: how solemn then the thought, that we mortals erect to Him a dwelling, devote to Him a spot on his earth as a particular sanctuary. Let us however resort as usual to the Creator's own teaching, to his Scriptures, to see what they tell us, and connect therewith the remarks proper for this occasion. When Solomon had built his house to the Mighty One of Jacob, when

---

* Spoken at the dedication of the synagogue at Washington, D. C., Friday afternoon, July 30th, 5623.

it stood there in all its splendour and glory, he even then felt the inadequacy of human labour to be properly acceptable to God, and thus he spoke in the words which we have just read:*

"For in truth will God then dwell on earth? behold, the heavens and heavens of heavens cannot contain Thee, how much less then this house which I have built." 1 Kings viii. 27.

Indeed, if we inquire of human reason, whether it would be proper to erect a house for the residence of the divine glory, we should be induced to pretermit our intention; since the Incorporeal cannot be confined within any limits; and thus we would never dedicate any houses to the worship of God, as the wide space of the plains, and the expanse of ocean are equally his with all the structures human ingenuity can contrive. Wherever we turn our view, we have the Lord's possessions before us, we ourselves are a portion of his wealth. Nothing of which we have a conception as existing but belongs to the Lord; wherefore we can give Him nothing, nor dedicate to him aught that is not HIS already. But we Israelites do not govern ourselves by reason only, we resort for instruction to the revelation which has been communicated to us from Sinai, and there we find it recorded that we are permitted to erect houses to the name of God, where we are promised that He will be more immediately among us than elsewhere, in a manner which we cannot explain. So also with re-

---

* I had just read, as a part of the dedicatory service, 1 Kings viii. 22–44.

gard to prayer: the Omniscient is conscious of all our wants before we arrange even our thoughts into entreaty; our words are not needed to enlighten his understanding of our requirements and hopes; wherefore cold human reason would likewise absolve us from the duty of prayer as useless and presumptuous. But revelation teaches us by the words of Deut. iv. 7: "For what great nation is there that hath gods so nigh unto it, as is the Lord our God at all times that we call upon Him?" that we should apply to our Father above in all relations of life in the words of prayer, in order that we may be relieved of our burden, and obtain his almighty aid. We therefore are permitted to erect houses, not to inclose the illimitable One within limits, but to have a home for his law, where we may assemble to be instructed in order to feel the influence of his divine spirit; we are allowed to pray, in order that we may be convinced that our enlargement is not the result of our skill and labour, but the immediate effect of the providence of the Lord, through whose beneficence we exist. We therefore, as permitted by the highest Authority, dedicate these walls as a house of assembly for the children of Israel dwelling in this place, that from it the law may go forth, and they may be enlightened with regard to the deeds they should perform, and encourage each other to be true to the law which has been confided to us as our inheritance, which hitherto has been and hereafter shall be transmitted as the heirloom of the congregation of Jacob. Though thus the law is primarily our own property, it was not confided to us for our exclusive benefit. When it was proclaimed from the summit of Horeb, while the heavenly fires blazed out with intense brightness, and outward nature was convulsed to its centre, the world lay shrouded in the deepest gloom. Knowledge of Truth was nowhere; in every direction were falsehood and superstition worshipped, while the rights of man were disregarded by all governments, and irreligion and tyranny ruled hand in hand. But when the Lord in his might had broken our chains, and led us through his messenger Moses to the foot of Horeb, He himself enlightened our understanding, and not in uncertain and painful researches, but in a direct and audible manner He made the truth known to us, when He spoke these significant words: "I am the Eternal thy God who have brought thee out of the land of Egypt, from the house of bondage." Wise men of many nations, especially among the Greeks and Romans, such as Socrates, Plato, Aristotle, and Cicero, painfully strove to know what God is; but they always failed, though often they approached the truth. And so it would have been yet, had men been left to search for the precious truth unaided. But when our fathers were assembled to receive the law, with their wives and little ones, their servants and maid-servants, their hewers of wood and drawers of water, their understanding was in a moment instructed in the highest truth, and they were taught that all this vast universe, these seas and rivers, these plains and mountains, these stars and planets, these constellations and suns in their infinite courses around which other planets than our own revolve, the material and spiritual, sprung from the creative word of the One and only God, whose visible glory was then made manifest to their outward eyes, and whose law was indelibly fixed in their hearts forever. For the standard of truth, placed in their hands at that time and that place, has been preserved by them through all the vicissitudes they have had to encounter, and neither joys nor sorrows have been able to unloose their hold thereof, and it is theirs this day, of which the assembly present is the witness; since the house in which we are is devoted to the same Eternal One who made his will and his name known to our ancestors in the desert of Horeb.

If men should now question us as to what we have done for the collective mass of mankind? we will answer them, that we have been faithful guardians of the divine truth, the first promulgators of universal charity, the first to set a barrier to tyranny, and the first to base the happiness of society on equitable laws, protecting equally the rights of all classes of the inhabitants of the land. We have not been distinguished, it is true, for our discoveries in philosophy, nor for our achievements in arms, nor in the pleasant fields of poetry and the fine arts, nor have we enriched the world by our inventions, especially not of the destructive engines of war; in this Greeks and Romans, and Spaniards and Englishmen, and other modern people have been our superiors; but our contribution to the common stock has been the highest for the welfare of mankind, as it embraces the elements of humanity and civilization, far exceeding in value all the others enumerated, and destined to produce yet more glorious results than have been witnessed hitherto. Thirty-five centuries have elapsed since this code was communicated; but every passing moment adds its testimony to its exceeding worth, and the deeper men enter into the mysteries of science, the more will they become convinced of its truth and beauty. And whether it is recognized or not, it underlies the legislation of all civilized states, and the closer its precepts are followed, the better will human happiness be promoted. At its first inception it overcame the idols of Egypt, while their worshippers were compelled in the agony of their suffering to acknowledge the supremacy of the Mighty One of Israel. The process of time, on the other hand, beholds the triumphant advance of the Scriptures; for whether they are in the original language, as with us, or in one of the many tongues spoken by men, they are steadily chasing away the gloom of mental darkness from the human mind, and implanting gradually the soothing principles of universal love which they inculcate. For go into the cathedral of the Catholic, the church of the Episcopalian, the meeting-house of the Dissenter, or the mosque of the Mahomedan, and you will hear propounded doctrines which sprung from our law; and though they may not have come from us directly, they are nevertheless an emanation from the same source whence we derive our guide of life: and thus we utter no idle boast when we maintain, that the civilizing principle which is gradually spreading over the earth came from us as its centre, and we have performed a true service to all men, by preserving the law during all the trials which we had to endure, in order to retain it pure and undefiled as we had received it. Whatever morality exists is moreover clearly traceable to our own; no practical rule of life has been invented or developed which has not its origin in our code; if therefore modern society is in advance of the ancient, it is only in the degree that it has been directed by the Hebrew element of civilization in which the other was deficient.

The prejudice which has been excited against us in all ages is thus proven to be extremely unjust; for instead of our being a burden on society, we have been its greatest benefactors. And still how long is it since we were spurned everywhere as enemies and outcasts? Who in the Middle Ages had pity on the Jew? who commiserated his fallen condition? Turn whither he would, he was met by persecution; in Spain, in France, in England, in Germany, in Italy, everywhere he was pursued by the fanatical hatred of princes, priests, and people; every one thought himself at liberty to maltreat him for some fancied offence against state and individuals, which was foreign to his heart and feeling. Nevertheless, he bore it all with patience, because he endured it in the defence of that priceless law which had been intrusted to his safe keeping. And he has lived to see the Scriptures diffused all over the earth, and to hear everywhere rising on High the Psalms and prayers of his own royal poet, those of his great teacher, Moses the man of God, and of the other sweet singers whom his nation has produced; and the words of admonition, addressed to the people from thousands of pulpits, are based on texts drawn from his prophets, his historians, and his moralists, who thus rule the minds of the present nations of the earth, though they are almost unconscious whence the light comes in which they bask, or whence emanate the high-toned principles which are the governing rules of their life.

Thus, though we have been reviled, and spurned, and excluded from human sympathies, we stand here unconsumed this day in the capital of the Western world, and dedicate this house to the sole, eternal, ever-existing Almighty God, whose dwelling is the universe, and whose spirit pervades all time and space. The dimensions are not indeed vast, the ornaments are truly not gorgeous; but will anything human hands have contrived be a fit offering to the Most High? There are the church erected by Buonaroti, that of Peter at Rome, and the work of the great Wren, that of Paul in London, the Madeleine in Paris, and of Isaac in Petersburgh, and other magnificent basilikas and cathedrals as they are called; but are they worthy dwellings of the One whom the heavens cannot contain, as Solomon said when he had finished the great work on which the wealth and skill of his age had been exhausted? No, friends, it is not the size and elegance of the building which will please the Lord of all, but the spirit of the worshippers: if this be in accordance with his will, then shall we experience abundance of peace and consolation in our assemblies, and He will indeed come unto us and bless us. If then you, my brother Israelites, wish truly to hallow these walls, show yourselves worthy of your kindred, and let this house be the means to kindle in you a true devotion to the Eternal God, the Mighty One of Jacob and his Redeemer, even the Lord who released your ancestors from Egyptian bondage, to be to Him a perpetual inheritance and the undying witnesses of his being, that He is God!

While we thus claim the respect of the world for our opinions and conduct in accordance with them, we cannot deny, and wish not to conceal it, that we are in an antagonistic position with the vast majority of mankind. Though they have derived their religion from the Bible, they have not adopted the One Lord as the God of their worship. They believe in a divided godhead, or, as they term it, in a triune God, while we believe in an absolute Unity, without a possible division of persons or powers, having full faith that all the acts of God are manifestations of the same undivided, indivisible One, who is at the same time Creator, Governor, and Saviour of all whom He has called into being. But while we thus boldly dissent, we are not permitted to hate or persecute another for differing from us in opinion. The religion we profess we conceive to be our peculiar inheritance; but we deny the hope of salvation to no one who fulfils the duties of humanity which are incumbent on all men alike. If you are then told that Israelites have ever been persecutors of their fellow-men, do not believe it; we never forced our faith on others; and the few instances which are recorded against us, and which apparently prove the contrary, can easily be explained so as to remove the charge from us when it is clearly presented; but I have not time enough to-day to enter into a discussion which would, besides, be foreign to my present object. All that is necessary now is to enter an emphatic denial against the assumptions often made, and which have been employed to justify the horrible cruelties inflicted on us, for our adherence to the faith of our ancestors. For our part, however, though we are fully convinced of the truth of our belief, which excludes confidence in any other, and prevents us to give our assent to any other, we do not presume to limit the mercy of God. He has bestowed on us his law, by which alone we can obtain salvation; it was given to us to guard it against all assaults, under all circumstances; but this authorizes us not to exclude from our kindness those who are not inheritors of this religion. We should emulate herein his ways of mercy. He is a universal God, and his sun shines equally for the Turk and Hindoo as for the Hebrew, and his rain falls on sea and dry land, and refreshes the barren wastes of Siberia, as well as the fertile plains of America, and the deserts of Arabia no less than the savannas of the new world. Everywhere the evidences of his bounty meet our eyes. Why, then, shall we hate and injure those who have not been taught as we have been? Why should not one human being tolerate all who share not his convictions? Still we will not conceal that we look forward for the time when the holy Name whom we adore shall be sanctified by the mouth of all men; when the veil shall be removed from all eyes, which shall see the divine glory revealed unto them with that certainty and undying conviction as was done to our fathers, when they marched forth into the wilderness to enter on their wonderful pilgrimage through the whole course of the world's history. But in the words of the prophet Zechariah (iv. 6): "Not by might, nor by power, but by my spirit, saith the Lord of hosts." We do not look forward to triumph by the might of armed hosts, nor by political power, neither of which we can wield, but the spirit which was intrusted to us in days of yore, which will prevail with all the sons of men as it has prevailed with us, sanctifying as it progresses, becoming firmer as it advances, till every thing will yield willingly before its all-conquering power.

We have given you thus, my non-Jewish hearers, a brief sketch of our faith, and of the views which we entertain towards those who differ from us. Let me now appeal to you to discard the unworthy prejudices which many have been taught to entertain against us. Excluded so long from the sympathies of mankind, it is but natural that many of us should have acquired habits not altogether commendable. But it is wrong to charge this fault upon all Israelites, as though all had sinned. The name of Jew has even become unjustly a term of reproach, although it has an honourable origin; since Leah when she had borne his fourth son to Jacob, called him Judah (whence the name of Jew was by various changes derived), "because this time will I thank the Lord," feeling grateful for the favour of being the mother of so many sons of the patriarch. We may have lost much of our ancient high character through the course of so many terrible sufferings. But the heart of the Hebrew is still the seat of kindness; distress always appeals to him in tones he cannot resist, and few of us are ever guilty of violent robbery or of imbruing their hands in a fellow-man's blood. Even when we were expelled from our homes, and were forced to wander abroad in misery and poverty, we turned not round on our assailants and plunged our dagger into their heart. The banner which we received from Sinai has not been stained by treason; yet its white folds bear many a mark of blood, but it issued from the wounds in our own heart; the life-gore of Israel's sons and daughters has left there its fearful traces, and it was trailed through the pool which came from the wounds inflicted in our bosoms by the deadly weapons of our adversaries, who slew without mercy those who would not relinquish their belief to the demands of those who for the time bore rule over them, and whose favour could easily have been conciliated, had they consented to forsake the God of their fathers, and united themselves with those around them. We also as a class are faithful to the governments under which we live; and although until lately we were nearly everywhere excluded from the rights of citizenship and debarred from all offices, men belonging to our communion have fallen on the battle-fields of contending nations, even where the combat was not for the rights of man, but the ambition of opposing potentates. And in the fearful struggle which now afflicts this land, our victims have not been wanting, who hastened to embark their lives and fortunes at the call of the authorities. Our hearts always pulsate with the purest and noblest sentiments, and we will not teach our children to hate their fellow-men. We will indeed tell them how much we suffered from persecution, what cruelties were causelessly inflicted on us; yet not that they might hate others, but that they may be induced to love with deep affection that sacred legacy for which so many laboured, for which so many suffered, that it might be preserved untarnished for them and their descendants forever, and to bring pure civilization to all mankind. We will teach them the holy precepts of the Scriptures: "And thou shalt love the Lord thy God with all thy heart, with all thy soul, and all thy might," and "Thou shalt love thy neighbour as thyself," that they may fulfil their highest duty to their God on high, and to their fellow-beings who dwell near them on earth. For it is charity alone which can accomplish our mission; the tree of life cannot flourish in the midst of violence; truth can be nursed only by the arts of peace.

But we have also a hope for the future. We confidently expect that the time will come when warfare and oppression will cease everywhere; when peace shall reign triumphant under the rule of the Prince Messiah, whom the Lord will send to govern mankind by the law of kindness, "the breath of whose lips shall slay the wicked," as Isaiah says, meaning that no carnal weapon will henceforth be needed to enforce justice and protect the innocent. And as Ezekiel (xxxiv. 25) says: "And they shall dwell in the wilderness in safety, and sleep in the forests." Who can now lie down in safety in the depth of the forest? is he not in danger from the fang of the poisonous serpent? the claws of the bloodthirsty tiger? the talons of the lordly lion? and more yet from the cunning and malice of his fellow-man, who lies in wait for him to rob him of his treasures, or to aim at his life? Yet at that glorious time all shall be peace and safety; but it will only be when the law of God has conquered all hearts, and the name of the Lord is revered in all the earth.

You, my Hebrew friends! I have to admonish solemnly to do honour to the name you bear; to prove by your conduct that you wish truly to consecrate this house, by an observance of the Sabbaths and festivals, by an honourable course of life as men and citizens, by training your children in the way they should go, and by showing in your whole conduct that you are sincere in your attachment to the law of Heaven; so that God's spirit may come and sanctify this house, and cause light and instruction to proceed thence unto many who may come hither to worship. And let us pray that the time may speedily arrive, when the Name of the Lord shall be adored as the only One from the rising of the sun to the setting thereof, and that all mankind, thus joining in the worship of the Pure and Holy, and united in bonds of love and kindness, may give thanks and glory to the God of Israel, and join in one universal Amen Hallelujah.

NOTE.—The above address was entirely extemporaneous, and made up after the speaker had taken a survey of his audience, which was largely composed of non-Israelites; wherefore he deemed it his duty to utter a defence of practical Judaism, the first time it was possible for him to do so in the capital of the Union, and he trusts that it may not have been entirely without some good result.

DISCOURSE XI.

THE LAW TESTED.*

BRETHREN!

In the present state of agitation which pervades the public mind, it is advisable that the thinking Israelite should reflect well on the evidences of his religion. He will find himself assailed, and his opinions

---

* Being the substance of a sermon delivered at the Synagogue Beth El Emeth, on Sabbath Nitzabim-Vayelech, 5624.

subjected to a close criticism; wherefore he must be prepared to satisfy himself not less than others that he is in possession of the truth. If our system were simply the product of modern days, or a mere human invention, it might not be of such absorbing importance to investigate and defend it; but we claim for it another origin, and, therefore, cannot consent to let ourselves be deprived of the same by any agency whatever; and as the human mind is apt to indulge in doubts, we should take heed that we may obtain the means to remove them, that they may not permanently influence our thoughts and actions.

If a thing is true, it is not so only for the time being, but in all other conceivable periods. If the law of Israel was, therefore, true at the time it was promulgated, it must be so now, and at any period hereafter; and if we can show that in its details it has proved itself true, that it has announced nothing which time has overthrown: we may freely dismiss all misgiving, and avow our steady adherence to the same.

The lesson which we have read this day, from the Pentateuch, embraces the last admonition which Moses addressed to the people of Israel before his decease; as he only spoke yet the admirable song which he intrusted to the priests and Levites, and the blessings which he bestowed on the various tribes, when he ascended the mount of Nebo, where he ended his mortal career. In this admonition he told the people what the future would bring forth for them. He warned them against transgressing the law, and at the same time announced that, in case they were to do so, the direst punishments should befall them nationally and individually; for that the disregard of the divine precepts would assuredly draw after it "all the curses that are written in that book of the law" which he had just completed, and given into the custody of the people as their common and permanent property. He foresaw the commonwealth of Israel disrupted by internal rottenness, consequent on an abandonment of the path which he had been the means of marking out for the guidance of the people: still he said, in connexion with the work he was about completing, that it should be written down for a memorial,—

כי לא תשכח מפי זרעו :

"For it shall not be forgotten out of the mouth of his seed." Deut. xxxi. 21.

Was this an idle boast? Was it merely a love for his own institutions which induced Moses thus to speak? If so, the events of history would have contradicted him, and proved that his assertion was false; the effect, at most, of a life-long devotion to a cause which he had espoused, but nothing more. Yet what has the world witnessed in this respect? Has the law of Moses, as it is called, perished? or, rather, has the divine revelation of Sinai ceased out of the mouth of Abraham's descendants? By no means; trials of joy and tribulation have alternated for thousands of years; obedience to our religion at one time and disobedience at another have characterized Israel, and still the law is unforgotten. We lived respected and powerful in our land, under the banner of our faith, and we have been plucked thence by the violent hand of gentile invaders, and still the code of Sinai is unforgotten. The prediction, therefore, has not the character of an enthusiastic excitement, but that of an absolute certainty, which has been confirmed by the experience of mankind.

The Israelites have well understood also the task which this divine inheritance has imposed on them; they have not rested satisfied with the mere possession of it, they have, on the contrary, done everything to perpetuate it among themselves. They have made it their daily study and their nightly meditation. Every act of their lives has reference to its spirit and teaching, and it thus has become incorporated with their very being. It is constantly perused both at home and in our public assemblies; and once a year, thus have our wise men ordained, should it be read through, assigning a portion to every Sabbath, that it may be kept unceasingly fresh in our memory. We may have heard the lesson before, but still it comes ever with the force of a new conviction to enlighten our understanding. We are not, however, to content ourselves with having the weekly lesson read to us in synagogue only, but we should previously at home compare the text with a translation, that the words, when proclaimed in public, shall not fail to make their full impression on our mind. It requires no long argument to prove both the propriety and the necessity of the reading of the law as we do. If we were to parcel it out in small sections, and consume years in its perusal, is it not likely that the law might gradually fade from our memory? If there were no incentive to study it, it would be neglected; and when the practice of religion should have become slack, the very existence of the precepts might be forgotten. The general knowledge our people always have had of their faith is mainly due to their constant reading of the Torah; it became familiar to them from their infancy, without any particular trouble or exertion, and the continual annual repetition of the instruction in their presence suffered at no time the impression on their memory to fade away, and thus the youth and the hoary head had the same knowledge and the same incentive to act, and to remain faithful to the same standard. Understand, it is not merely the hearing of the text in Hebrew which has effected this, or can do so hereafter, it is the understanding of what is read alone which can produce any good result; hence the necessity for imparting a knowledge of the holy language, that it may be familiar to our people, so that they can listen to it with understanding and pleasure. But even when this is not attainable, the facilities have been provided by our pious and learned men to render the Scriptures accessible to all, without distinction of class; from the earliest period of our exile efforts have been made, and this with the greatest success, to make the sense of the holy Word clear to the commonest intellect, and all who will, can approach the sacred fountain and satisfy their thirst for knowledge. Thus has Judaism not been at any time the property of any favoured caste; no one had to unlock the holy treasure for the community at large; for all were the common owners of the inheritance of Jacob, and could and did participate in its benefits. The reading, accordingly, of the law and the sections of the prophets, as a part of our devotional exercises, is a vital matter to our religious life, since the Scriptures are the source of our belief and practice; wherefore, the utmost possible acquaintance with them is needed to enable us to accomplish the problem of our existence; and the incentive imparted by their being publicly proclaimed on all Sabbaths, fasts, and festivals, must induce the people at large to desire to become constantly more thoroughly familiar with them. We hold the simple Word itself more powerful and efficacious than all comments and the most eloquent appeals of the orator; it speaks to the believer in the tones of conviction, and he requires nothing else to stimulate him to follow the path which his fathers have trodden before him for many generations. But, if you banish the law as too troublesome to be listened to, and tell the people that a short lesson now and then is all that is needed to remind them of its existence, can you expect that the ancient familiarity of Israelites with it will continue? that our people will not degenerate to the practical unacquaintance with it, which is so strikingly the case with our gentile neighbours? They have a far more superficial knowledge of our law than we have, though they have the same Bible; but if you pursue the same course regarding it, you will sink rapidly to their level, and prepare gradually the way of forgetting it likewise. The practice handed down to us is the one which both safety and prudence must recommend, and let us endeavour to contribute our share, every one, by becoming thoroughly imbued with its letter and spirit, that the "law may not be forgotten from the mouth of our latest descendants."

This reminds me of the labor of the Massorites,

the men who devoted their lifetime to the illustration and fixing of the holy Text. They counted the verses, words, and letters of the Scriptures, and left us directions how they were to be written and read. Some may think it a trifling with sacred things, to inform you gravely how many times a certain word or letter recurs in the Bible. But reflect, on the other hand, that if we have clear directions how our forefathers wrote and preserved the Scriptures, we have an infallible guide to demonstrate at any time the falsehood of any pretended additions which any one may offer for our acceptance. The record of these critical notes, called the Massorah, is thus the most valuable criterion which can be devised for the maintenance of the purity of the divine revelation, and we have in this wise been enabled to preserve it pure and unsullied throughout the long ages of persecution which we had to encounter. Should ever, by any combination of circumstances, all the Hebrew manuscripts be lost, the Massorah would enable us to restore the text in all its perfection. For the very grammatical deviations, as some consider them, are parts of the text as received by us, and are noted as correct in this traditional criticism, and are, therefore, necessary to complete the Bible, and to render it just so as our fathers have left it to us. We must, accordingly, admire the singleness and simplicity of their devotion for the truth, that they laboured so zealously and at the same time so successfully to hand down to the latest generations, unabridged and unaltered, the divine legacy as they had received it, and with such safeguards as will protect it, provided it is kept free from foreign intermeddling, against all assaults of the forger and falsifier in times to come. It thus happened that, even in those ages when books could be multiplied only by the slow and laborious process of manuscript copying, the Hebrew Scriptures maintained their remarkable uniformity to such an extent, that no reasonable man can doubt the identity of the text from the most remote period with that now in our possession; and it was, under Providence, all the work of those vigilant teachers who taught the people the facts and words of the Bible, so that they became incorporated with the very being of Israel, and could, therefore, not be forgotten. It was thus that in the darkest periods of persecution and general ignorance, the Israelites were always an educated and enlightened people, and far above the average of their contemporaries; and though at present literature has received, by means of the printing art, the greatest diffusion, let us not despise and esteem lightly the instrument and the men who served us so well and so disinterestedly in the hour of trial, although the great multiplication of copies of the Scriptures seems to secure us against the danger of forgetting them utterly, or of accepting spurious editions as the correct transcript of the Divine Word. For even on the score of prudence, it is advisable to be armed against all contingencies, so as to be ready with the best means of defence when they may have to be called into effective service, and to guard our sacred treasure against all interpolations, additions, or arbitrary amendments, which may be proposed at any time hereafter.

The law, being thus the inheritance of Jacob's children, might have preserved them perpetually in their national character and in their own country as an independent people. But they chose to neglect their own happiness, in their desire to adopt the freedom from restraint which they witnessed among their gentile neighbours; perhaps the general prosperity which they had enjoyed undermined their morals, and they therefore indulged in matters which the law interdicted. What Moses had foretold unto them occurred: hostile nations invaded the land of Palestine, and one portion after the other was swept clear of its population, and we learned too late the difference between. bearing the easy yoke of Heaven to wearing the chains which our conquerors fastened on our limbs. And we then went forth into captivity, and on the banks of the streams of Babylon we hung up our once tuneful harps, and it was in vain that our captors demanded of us to waken their mute chords with the songs of Zion. How could we sing the solemn melodies which filled formerly the courts of the temple, when the joyous multitudes of the sons of Israel had assembled to worship the Most High? Was not his house a desolate heap? Were not his priests banished from their station? Were not the people of God driven forth into exile and bondage for their manifold transgressions? No, our song was hushed, and on the soil of the stranger the once free heart of Judah refused to respond to the demand of the conquerors, and we could not forget Jerusalem, the former crown of our glory. And thus again was the blessed promise fulfilled, that the law should not be forgotten from the mouth of our descendants. In Palestine we grievously offended our heavenly Father, we provoked Him by our misdeeds, we defied his anger; and when the threatened doom had befallen us, we turned back within ourselves, refused to seek consolation by amalgamating, like other conquered nations, with those who had subdued us. The law, the customs, the psalmody, all that characterized ancient Israel, became doubly dear to us, and from the wreck of our state we saved our religion, and it has accordingly preserved us intact and unconquerable to this day. And when the period of the Babylonian captivity had elapsed, a remnant returned to Palestine, and while rearing again the walls of the sacred edifice, we laid deeper and broader the foundations of our faith, and it has stood the test of the sorest trials which the world has ever witnessed, and it has survived, and it has sustained us in our separate national existence, the wonder and the envy of those who love not the name of Israel; and we have every reason to hope confidently, that no event hereafter will be able to effect what all preceding human exertions have failed to accomplish,—the obliteration of the law from the mouth and heart of Jacob's latest descendants.

We are thus here, brethren, at this distance of time, to avow our adherence to our holy and unforgotten Law, practically the same Israel as we were many centuries ago. The joyous events which were experienced in our history have not destroyed the strength of our national character; and the trials to which other people succumbed have, it is true, left their terrible traces, but they have not consumed us utterly, and we have preserved the testimony of God, uncorrupted and unchanged, as it was delivered to us by our great prophet, who, dying, constituted the whole people its guardians. And soon we shall enter on a new year, when we shall assemble again in the houses dedicated to God, to declare Him anew the glorious King of Israel and the Sovereign of the universe. But take heed that you bring not a false offering when you approach God's sanctuary; let your heart be in unison with your professions, and feel the greatness of the privilege in being permitted to adore the One who dwells to eternity. Reflect that when Moses had admonished his hearers, he gave them the choice between right and wrong, life and death, and urged them to choose life. He stood there as the representative of the Most High, and exclaimed, in the height of his inspired enthusiasm, "I call heaven and earth as witnesses against you this day, that I have set before you life and death, the blessing and the curse; therefore, choose thou life, in order that thou mayest live, both thou and thy seed." How noble an attestation! He did not adjure them by human love or mortal aspiration, not by anything man in his eager pursuit values or desires; but he called on the everlasting creatures of God to watch over the upholding of the Lord's covenant by the people to whom it had been intrusted. The everlasting Word is to be guarded by the creatures which are imperishable in their nature, unless destroyed by the Power which has called them forth; they survive nations and their works; they are always present to tell the glory of their Maker, and to proclaim his might and wisdom. If kingdoms rise, become powerful, and fall again into decay, the earth itself undergoes no change, it responds to the labour of man, and "giveth seed to the ploughman, and bread to the consumer." The seasons change in their regular course, and the ocean beats unceasingly against the shore, though navies have been engulfed in its waves. So does the sun shine for a perpetual light by day, and the sweet effulgence of the moon and the glitter of the stars guide the traveller by land and sea during the hours of night. Everywhere are these witnesses of God with us, and from the beginning their laws were established, which nothing can trespass. We speak of changes, of revolutions, of progress, and improvements; but the ordinances of nature, as decreed by the Almighty at the beginning, are still the same as they were when first implanted in all things. So it is fitting that they should testify to the eternal WORD which, spoken at Sinai, has sped onward on its mission, and still continues to enlighten the hearts of all believers. Whatever it has suffered has not weakened the force of its truth, and however often we have transgressed and rebelled, it has stood unmoved, despite of our unwillingness to labour for its advancement. Heaven and earth have not passed away, and the law also has survived all the shocks to which it has been subjected, unscathed and eternally the same.

Perhaps you may say that the earth and heaven are but silent creatures, and cannot speak, and are therefore improperly summoned as witnesses for or against any one. But it is only in a metaphorical sense that the prophet spoke, as though he could summon all nature to be present at the making of the everlasting covenant between God and Israel. We have already seen that the subject-matter was worthy of such a solemn appeal; God was giving a law to his people which was ultimately destined to win to itself, in some form, all the human family; but, in the meantime, we, its guardians, were to watch over it, that no danger might happen to it, while it guards ourselves against annihilation and from being swallowed up among the masses of mankind. And everywhere at this day are the witnesses whom Moses invoked present. When we till the soil, there is the earth as it was in ages gone by, ready to respond to our labour, and to yield its increase for our bodily sustenance. When we look abroad over the green fields or flowery meadows, behold the limpid stream or the rushing cataract, we are greeted by the same phenomena which once delighted the eye of the great seër of Israel. When we direct our look upward, and behold the sun, and moon, and the starry host of heaven, and contemplate the countless worlds which blaze nightly in the skies, standing like sentinels in the vast field of nature forever: we have there the same mighty works of God which were called on to testify when Israel listened to the man who, on the brink of eternity, thought only of his mission, to leave an eternal light to the people whom he had been selected to lead away from bondage to freedom. And when the sky is overcast by thick clouds, and rain descends on the earth, and anon the curtain is lifted, and the rays of the setting sun shine through the pearly drops, by which the bow of promise is reflected on the vault of heaven, think of Him who has made a covenant with our fathers that the flood shall no more pass over the earth to destroy all flesh, as had been done in the days of Noah. This covenant with man and animated creatures has been faithfully kept; and though the earth has been polluted by the sins of its inhabitants, the surging waves of the flood have never been since then permitted to destroy all flesh. And, like the covenant of the rainbow, stands the covenant of the law. Indestructible in its character, the divine promise has been maintained in both instances; and while the earth has not ceased to have its seedtime and harvest, its summer and winter, its heat and cold, its night and day; while the beautiful colours of the rainbow, the sign of the covenant, ever and anon reflected by a law of nature which changes not, remind us of the truth and faithfulness of our heavenly Father; the existence of Israel as a people, the fact that the law has not been forgotten thus far from the mouth of its latest descendants, the continual shining of the divine light in the atmosphere of human history, will and must convince us that our religion has stood the test, which the prophet proposed to prove its truth; and we are justified to assert, in the sincerity of conviction, that we have guarded the truth which had been intrusted to us for safe-keeping forever, even while the earth stands on its basis, and the heavens declare in their unheard melody the glory of the everlasting God.

Whenever, then, parents are blessed with offspring who have arrived at the age* when they become members of the congregation of Israel, let them rejoice that they have been permitted to rear new bearers of the heavenly testimony, and to maintain and propagate the inheritance of Jacob. Let them be glad that they can offer such a sacrifice to the cause of truth, future champions of Judaism, who are to carry forward the message of truth, when its present

---

* Referring to a Bar Mitzvah then in synagogue.

witnesses are laid in the grave to sleep in death till the time of the re-awakening. For it was for this object that we were selected from all people, that we might be ever present to testify that the word of God is imperishable; and we have not ceased to be, because of the promise to our fathers, which has upheld us, and preserved us to this day. Let also the young sons of Israel rejoice that they have been born of a race whose God is the Lord, and that they have become through their birth the inheritors of everlasting truth, the eternal life which the Lord of all has implanted within us.

And you all, who are of the seed of Israel! rouse yourselves to the holy work which has been confided to you. Attune your hearts, not to the sound of music, but to the harmony which dwells in imperishable truth, to serve the Lord with all your heart. Consecrate your spirits to the service of the Most High, and take heed that not one of your friends, children, or dependents, shall become untrue to the religion of your fathers by your own acts or omissions. Teach, exhort, instruct, by your words and example, that all within your reach may be brought within the circle of God's servants, the defenders of the divine testimony, which is our common property; and let us all, when we acknowledge, on the coming New Year, the Lord as the Eternal King, and invoke Him as the Father of Mercy, not honour Him with our lips only, but let our spirit in its innermost recesses feel in full force that He is indeed our God, and that his word is the only guide which can lead us safely, now and forever, through the dangers of life. And may He in his goodness send us his blessing in the coming year, and bring us near to his service, so that we may be enabled to sanctify his name, and proclaim his wonders which He has shown to us and our fathers. Amen.

DISCOURSE XII.

HOW TO MOURN.*

BROTHERS AND FRIENDS!

The event which has induced you to send for me, in order to appear before you to-day to become in a measure the interpreter of your feelings and sympathy with your fellow-citizens, is well calculated to arrest the attention of all by its suddenness and significance. It tells us how frail is the tenure which we have on life, how brief are our days, how imminent is the close thereof, even when least expected. A similar misfortune befell the first high-priest of our people, Aaron, the brother of Moses, when he was bereft of his eldest two sons on one day, at the very period when they had been solemnly installed into the priestly office to the Most High, to serve in the sanctuary for the people of Israel. And we read in respect to this, in this day's section of the law:

ויאמר משה אל אהרן הוא אשר דבר ה׳ לאמר
בקרבי אקדש ועל פני כל העם אכבד וידם אהרן :

---

* Substance of an address spoken in the Synagogue of the Washington City Hebrew Congregation, on Sabbath, April 22d, 5625, a week after President Lincoln's violent death.

"And Moses said to Aaron, This is what the Lord hath spoken, saying, Through those who come near to me will I be sanctified, and before all the people will I be honoured; and Aaron remained silent." Lev. x. 3.

Let us endeavour to analyze these words of our great teacher. On that day the people had beheld the final consecration of a class of men selected from themselves to represent them in the sanctuary; the act was complete, and Aaron and his sons had been set apart for the everlasting priesthood. They had literally been brought nearer to God than their former associates; they alone could enter the holy place, and there perform the duties which they had to administer for the whole house of Israel. But it was precisely at this time, when they had just commenced their sacred functions, that death arrested two of them, and "they died before the Lord," meaning that they had offended by introducing, as our text says, unholy fire near the altar, and therefore they died suddenly, though otherwise in robust health. The people had thus, as Moses told his brother, an exemplification, that no position in life insures us immunity, and that the higher we rise in the scale of existence, the nearer we are to retribution. The priests of God had done only a slight wrong, according to human judgment; but, in their case, it had become a grave transgression, and their life paid the forfeit for their iniquity. Men are so apt to complain of the hardship of their fate—of the burdens they have to bear; and they look with envy on those who are raised above them, who occupy the high positions in society, and they fancy that the others are unduly favoured, while they are unjustly neglected. But when they see that those who are worthy and righteous, who are great and exalted, are exposed to the common lot of mankind, that these are not screened against punishment when they transgress: the Lord is sanctified by all, who will then acknowledge that He is just and impartial, and that human elevation only places us nearer to a rigid accountability. The humble will not therefore complain of the evils they have to encounter, seeing that all are alike subject to the mishaps incident to humanity; and in the fate which befalls the prominent in virtue, talents, and usefulness, they discover that there is no injustice or favouritism in the heavenly tribunal. When, therefore, those who are nearest to God feel the weight of divine indignation, the Lord himself is acknowledged as the just Ruler and the impartial Sovereign of the world, and all will ascribe to Him honour and glory, as the One who, exalted above all, watches over all with paternal solicitude, so that every one may meet with the recompense due to his deeds. Aaron felt the justice of this instruction thus solemnly conveyed to him by his prophet-brother, and remained silent in his deep sorrow, under the full conviction, that what he then suffered was for his and the people's ultimate good. But do not imagine that Aaron's submission was the result of indifference; on the contrary, the whole tenor of the narrative, and his refusal to eat the flesh of the sin-offering, according to the usual ordinance, proved that his father's heart was deeply grieved. And how could it have been otherwise? He had been associated with Moses in effecting the redemption of the Israelites; together they had gone to Pharaoh, to demand the freedom of their brothers, and he had stood alongside of him, till this wonderful deliverance was completed by the bestowal of the law from Sinai through the mediation of the greatest of prophets. While, however, Moses had been made the chief instrument of Israel's redemption, to Aaron and his descendants had been promised the priesthood as an inheritance to them forever. Moreover, by the divine grace the punishment for the defection at the making of the golden calf had just been remitted, and the people reinstated into favour, since God had accepted their liberal offerings from which the tabernacle and all its vessels had been constructed. Nay more, for a week previous, and up to that day, the sanctuary had been solemnly anointed and the sacrifices daily offered on the altar; and at length he himself had been admitted to bring the sacrifices, and his sons had aided him for the first time in their sacred functions; he had lifted up his hands to the people and blessed them, when, in token of the forgiveness of the national sin, the glory of God had been manifested to all the people; and all was gladness, and the shout of joy was lifted up simultaneously from the assembled faithful, and, to all appearance, there was nothing to disturb the general pleasure, or to mar the happiness of the father's heart. It was, however, in the moment of this blessed repose that a sudden bereavement robbed Aaron of half of his progeny; for his two stricken sons left no children, and his hopes were almost crushed. But he rose superior to the severe trial of that dreadful moment, and submitted in silence to the decree of the Most High, who thus willed to be glorified by the death of those whose devotion and sincere piety had brought them near to Him.

But why should we, my friends, exhibit such terror at the approach of death, as so many do? so mourn for the fallen as though all hope were fled? What is our earthly life? What is death? We are born to be here for awhile, to be removed hence when our task is done. For awhile, I say, because the death of the body is not the end of our existence. Our body is indeed laid in the grave to moulder away into corruption. But the spirit which once animated us has not been thereby annihilated, and it will survive in the presence of the God who bestowed it on us, to await his call for a purer life. It is the seed, as it were, of immortality, which we intrust to the earth, to arise thence when the graves are opened at the day of the resurrection. So does the husbandman intrust to the earth the precious seed. Anon examine it, after it has been buried awhile, and its symmetry and beauty are gone, and it presents an outward corruption, as though its life were fled. Yet watch it well; it contains the germ of a new existence, and soon it will bring forth the new plant to bear the seed, a hundredfold multiplied, to reward the labour of man. So also is death the door to eternal existence, purified and renewed, through the agency of material dissolution. Nothing is annihilated, only the form is changed, and all by the decree of the Supreme, who directs everything for our improvement. When, therefore, the righteous beholds the approach of death, when he feels that he must part with earth and its glories, he will not sink into dejection, nor dread the messenger who is to summon him hence, but await resignedly the stroke which is to cut asunder the thread of his earthly existence, and look with a well-founded trust to meet a paternal reception from our Father on high. On the other hand, those who are called on to mourn for the bereavement which death has wrought in their family-circle, should not complain as though they had been wronged by Providence, and weep without comfort, but submit with patience to the One who has removed the beloved friend, and acknowledge the justice of his decrees, which are always sent in mercy.

Though we may not be able to comprehend the ways of God, at the moment any event takes place, we may rest satisfied that all will ultimately have a happy result. We are not at liberty to say that God directs the hand of the assassin, or sends the robber to commit his violation on the property of others. But after the wicked have accomplished their work, which they meant for evil, Providence steps in, even to the satisfaction of our limited view, and directs all, so that no permanent injury shall be wrought thereby, and that the crime be deprived of the fatal consequences which the wrong-doer contemplated.

In the present affliction which has cast a deep shadow over the joy of the country, and arrested so suddenly the exultant shout which was heard but a week ago, we, as servants of the Lord, ought to turn our looks to Him, for guidance and strength. Let the sudden decease of the late President impress on us the important lesson, that all our joys are fleeting, all our prosperity is unstable. A week ago he was triumphant over those who had been in arms against the Union, of which he was the chief magistrate, and to-day his dead body is on its way to its final resting-place, and the grief of the people and the regret of the many cannot recall him from his slumber. While he was perhaps thinking of enjoying a period of tranquillity during his new term of office, after having had to witness strife and the tumult of arms during the first period of his presidency, when apparently the end of the struggle was nigh, and he might have anticipated a quiet and prosperous administration: the fatal messenger of death dashed down all these hopeful visions, and the chieftain rests suddenly from his labours. In place, however, of arraigning the mysterious ways of Providence, let us, like Aaron, submit meekly to what our strength cannot repair, which our wisdom cannot alter. When our first high-priest lost his two hopeful sons he did not rend his garments, he did not pull out his hair, he did not even break forth into the passionate words of grief like King David, "Oh, my sons! that I had died in your stead;" but silently, without uttering a solitary complaint, he yielded himself entirely to the divine behest, and bowed in submissive patience, though his paternal heart was ready to burst with the grief which it experienced. So let the American people likewise, in their present affliction, seek counsel from God; let them recognize Him in this hour of sorrow, and learn to put a proper value on the nothingness of human glory and the vanity of earthly power.—Mr. Lincoln had properly accomplished his mission; the work in which he had been engaged was nearly finished, and he could well leave it to others to fulfil what was still incomplete. He was taken away in the moment of triumphant success, and, so far as he was concerned, no additional length of days could have added to his greatness. If you were to ask a man how he would prefer to die, he probably would answer you, "Unexpectedly, and in the moment of success." Both these conditions accompanied Mr. Lincoln's decease; he was not conscious, not aware of the fatal blow which hurried him hence, and this at the moment of the highest success, before later occurrences, which might have happened, had caused him to feel disappointment in the incompleteness of the expected result. A thousand years added to his life would probably have failed to enhance his triumph. So far, therefore, as he is concerned, the people may well moderate their sorrow, and leave it to others to finish the work which the late chief had not yet fully ended.

But as regards ourselves, the death of Mr. Lincoln should not fail to teach us deep and solemn lessons. It should tell us not to cling so closely to earth and its joys, to pleasure, to power; since all are so readily taken from us. Let us rather consider ourselves as constantly subject to the divine summons, and be ready to meet them, as creatures of earth whose abode is not here. But I fear that the people have not properly appreciated these lessons. They appear to be excited to anger at the horrible crime which has been perpetrated, and to dwell too much on ideas of vengeance. I will admit that it is but just, at the first moment of such tidings as have been just flashed over the land, that men should indulge in detestation of the crime and abhorrence of the criminals; but with returning calmness, it is not proper to continue in this agitated frame of mind. It is not thus Mr. Lincoln's memory should be honoured. I have been told, since my arrival here, of several acts of personal kindness and clemency which it is said he delighted to indulge in. It is moreover said, that in the last cabinet council which he held with his chosen advisers, he expressed himself in terms of kindness towards the subdued public enemies, that it was his intention to pour the oil of conciliation on the troubled waves of war. Now, accepting the truth of this assertion, it were well that the people should forego their violent resentment, and imitate the goodness of heart evinced by their late President, and to let his example have a powerful influence towards inspiring them with sentiments of benevolence and forbearance. For behold, in the vast country to the southward from here the fierce desolations of a frightful war are everywhere visible. Cities have been ruined, fields rendered waste, homesteads levelled to the ground, and ruin stalks abroad over hill and valley. Deep are the traces of the havoc which armed hosts have wrought, and despair has seized on many inhabitants who have been driven forth bereft of their substance. Now is the time to let sweet peace smile again over the distracted land; to offer terms of conciliation to the conquered foes, so that hands which have been stretched forth armed with the deadly weapon to deal out death and destruction, may be soon held out again to grasp each other in token of a hearty reconciliation and restored friendship. But with the idea of vengeance, retaliation, and revenge, the future of the country will be sad indeed. The strife may be over, but peace cannot exist where mutual good-will is banished. And if men wish therefore to honour the memory of Mr. Lincoln, let them and their new ruler, on whom the grievous death of the one now mourned has devolved the government, imitate and follow up his merciful intention, and pour, as he had intended to do, the oil of kindness on the bleeding wounds of the land, to stifle the tumult of the feelings of the conquered, and induce them to again accept the control of the general government with cheerful acquiescence and unforced obedience.—But all mere noisy demonstration will be in vain; for soon will the image of the murdered President become tiresome to the masses to contemplate,—they will be unwilling to look at the fearful spectacle of the untimely slain, and all moral lessons which they ought to derive from the sad exhibition of human frailty will be lost on them, as though they had not been so terribly enforced; whereas, by dwelling on his good deeds and following his footsteps on the path of peace and conciliation, they will honour his memory truly, and be benefitted and improved by the instruction which the sudden bereavement should convey to us all, and they will act more in consonance with his naturally kind disposition, than by any loud demonstration of outward grief, which ends in forgetful indifference.

As regards the war in which Mr. Lincoln, as the chief magistrate of the Union, was engaged, permit me to pass it by, the time not having yet come to write its history impartially. The main features are known to you all, and their recital would convey no instruction to you, my hearers. Nor is this the place to discuss political subjects. But with respect to the moral view of the war, without trenching on the proximate political events which provoked it, we may freely say that SIN was the cause of it, yes, national sin was the cause of national strife. I will not specify any particular act which I might justly stigmatize as such; but surely there must have been grievous sinning which could enkindle so fearful a struggle, and we may freely say that a general discontent with the blessings here enjoyed contributed greatly to loosen the bonds of friendship which formerly united the various sections. But what ingratitude to the Bestower of all good does this dissatisfaction display! Behold the extent of the land! It stretches from the Atlantic to the Pacific Ocean, from the St. Lawrence to the Rio Grande; within this vast country, nearly as large as all Europe, you find the greatest variety of climate and soil. You find here the cotton, the sugar, the rice, the tobacco, the corn, the cereals of various kinds, and nearly all other productions of the soil which are needed for the sustenance of life and the outward comfort of man. Among the minerals you find the gold, the iron, the silver, the lead, the copper, the coal, and other substances which are calculated to embellish life and subserve the pursuits of arts and sciences. In respect to the liberty of the individual, this was fully secured by the fundamental law, the constitution of the land, which cast its ample protection over all the inhabitants, securing to them the right to acquire wealth, the pursuit of happiness without molestation from others, and the amplest religious freedom. And with all these blessings universally diffused, there still dwelt dissatisfaction in the hearts of many; and, therefore, we may assume, that God surrendered the people awhile to the control of their own passions, and we have beheld in consequence the fierce march of desolating strife and mutual slaughter, which we trust will soon be closed.

But the people must also repent, and turn their looks towards the Father who has for awhile abandoned them to themselves, and seek to govern themselves more in accordance with his revealed Word, and love mercy and righteousness, so that his wrath may be turned away, and He grant again peace and security to the now suffering land. But you, my Jewish hearers, have a special duty to perform in this connexion: you should, as the chosen servants of God, throw aside all defection from our religion of which you may be conscious. You must love the precepts which our Scriptures inculcate, and practise them on every occasion when the opportunity therefor presents itself, and thus contribute your share to cause the restoration of the divine favour to the country in which you have found a home for yourselves and your religion; and thus you will secure for yourselves the heritage of free institutions, in common with the citizens of other creeds, and obtain, as individuals, the especial blessing of your heavenly Father. For when you are called on to quit the earth, all the perishable goods for which you toiled, and which you prized so greatly, will not avail you aught; but virtuous deeds solely will plead for you to obtain from God pardon, grace, and mercy. If you then come laden with sin, the indignation of your omniscient Judge will demand of you a strict account as to the manner in which you have spent your days on earth, and how you have used the opportunities so often presented to you to acquire spiritual wealth; and the unrepentant sinner, the unpurified heart, will be doomed to that pain and punishment which it has merited by its obduracy and disobedience. But if you have sedulously obeyed the commands of the Lord, you can lie down calmly to sleep the sleep of death; for at the portals of eternity which you reach through the dissolution of your mortal portion, you will be received by your eternal Father, who will welcome back the returning child, and guard him forever in his fatherly protection. Salvation is within your own reach. Labour for it, and it will be yours, and while securing your own happiness, you will also benefit truly your fellow-men; since your example may incite them to imitate your conduct, and thus be the means of making them likewise pious and virtuous.

I have now to say a few words respecting the prayers that were offered up during our divine service for the repose of the soul of Mr. Lincoln. It is, indeed, somewhat unusual to pray for one not of our faith, but by no means in opposition to its spirit, and therefore not inadmissible. We pray for the dead, because we believe that the souls of the departed as well as of the living are in the keeping of God, and therefore the subjects of entreaty on our part, and of grace and pardon on that of our heavenly Judge. We also believe that, with very few exceptions, we cannot offend God eternally, so as to deserve eternal damnation; for we are taught כל ישראל יש להם חלק לעולם הבא, "All Israel have a share in the world to come;" wherefore temporary punishment will wipe away the sin committed in the flesh, after which the ransomed soul will be received in favour, having been redeemed through death and the purification of the punishment decreed against it. Again we are taught, חסידי אומות העולם יש להם חלק לעולם הבא, "The righteous of the nations of the world have a share in the life to come;"

and this, therefore, empowers us to pray for the rest in heavenly bliss for men of all nations, as our religion excludes from the favour of God no one who has done his will. The prayers, therefore, offered up this day for the deceased President are in accordance with the spirit of the faith which we have inherited as children of Israel, who recognize in all men those created like them in the image of God, and all entitled to his mercy, grace, and pardon, though they have not yet learned to worship and adore Him, as we do who have been especially selected as the bearers of his law. God will judge all according to the light they have received, and not withhold from them any reward their deeds have merited; while He will hold us to a strict accountability, if we, with the superior knowledge imparted to us, neglect the duties which our religion demands of us to perform.

One thing, among others, is obligatory on us, to do all in our power to promote the welfare of the country in which our lot is cast. We must honestly contribute to bear the burdens imposed on other citizens, and never offend against the laws enacted for the public security. Our religion makes no separation between us and men of other creeds. We should submit to the laws of the land in whatever does not militate against our moral and religious duties, though we had no part in their enactment. For so were we instructed by the prophet Jeremiah: "Build houses and dwell therein, and plant gardens and eat the fruit thereof; and seek the welfare of the city whither I have banished you, and pray for it unto the Lord; for in its welfare shall ye fare well." (Jer. xxix. 5, 7.)

This has nothing to do with our hope of the restoration of our own state; for while we are in banishment, we should strive to follow the instruction conveyed to us at a time when our absence from Palestine was limited to but seventy years. Be the time of our residence in a country long or short, we are commanded to seek its welfare, or peace, as the Bible calls it, peace, according to our acceptation, being the centre of all blessings; and to pray for the safety of the state, even as we do in all our religious assemblies, that the Lord may, in his goodness, protect the rulers of the land in the exercise of their functions, and grant peace to the country in which we live, and to the world at large. Peace, too, was the pursuit of Aaron, whose example of silent resignation we have dwelt on to-day; he is said to have been a lover and pursuer of peace, and that he did not confine his sacred office to administering on the altar, but he reconciled men who had a dispute, and restored harmony in the bosom of families. I cannot offer you a brighter example to follow. Be you also the promoters of peace; speak kindly of each other, mildly to each other, assuage angry passions wherever you see them displayed, and stay, if you can, the uplifted arm of violence from descending on the offender even. As citizens, contribute all in your power to the healing of the fearful effects of the late fratricidal strife, contribute by your efforts, as far as they may go, to obliterate the traces of war and the widespread desolation which afflicts so many of your countrymen, and breathe not of vengeance on the vanquished, convinced that by the acts of peace alone again cultivated, and the bonds of friendship again renewed, can this extensive land regain its prosperity, and resume its forward course, which the frightful series of battles has interrupted. But, above all, be strict adherents to your religion, practise all the duties it imposes on you; so that you may not, through your sinning, invoke punishment from on High on this land, where you have found a refuge and a free home for the exercise of your faith, so that you may live in security amid a peaceful and happy people, until that time when God will banish war and the instruments of war from the earth, when all men shall acknowledge Him solely as One and alone, in the days when He will send the Redeemer to rule over us in his name, even the Messiah the son of David. Amen.

NOTE.—After the address, the speaker offered up a prayer for the repose of the soul of the President; for consolation of the mourners; for the rulers of the land, that they might be guided to govern in wisdom and moderation, and be enabled to restore the country to peace and prosperity; for the congregation and its officers, that they might be permitted to govern, so as to secure its prosperity and promote godliness and brotherly love; and, finally, for all Israel, that we might live securely in the midst of the nations, unmolested by rulers and people, until the time of the Redeemer, when Israel shall again dwell in their own land, with the Lord Eternal for their God and King.

DISCOURSE XIII.

REVEALED TRUTHS.*

Brethren!

The religion which we profess, like all other systems of belief, is founded on certain principles, without which neither it nor any other could exist. Every religion, as it imposes duties on man which it expects he should observe, presupposes that there is a being, or that there are several beings, to whom he owes obligations; that there are certain acts which he must do to please the Deity, and that in case of non-obedience he is liable to inevitable evil consequences or, what is the same, punishments. These ideas, the existence of God, that of duties, whatever their nature may be, and of accountability, have therefore been called eternal, necessary, and absolute truths, or those which are unavoidable in any system of religion, and are founded so strongly on human reason that their admission is a matter of course, to contradistinguish them from others which Israelites claim as the basis of their belief, and which we will term revealed truths, or those which are not necessary, but are true because God has revealed them or made them known to us like other matters contained in the Bible. Some have attached greater importance to the first class of truths

---

* The substance of an address delivered at the synagogue Beth El Emeth, on Sabbath Vayiggash, Tebeth 5 (December 23), 5626.

than to the others, as they assert that their evidence is so striking, that man was by nature endowed with them, and it needed no direct interference of the Most High in order to impart them to mankind. It is true that nearly all nations which have come into contact with civilized peoples have, on their first discovery, shown that they had some notion of God, or rather that they invested some invisible or tangible being with some sort of superior power and authority; also that they had some sort of ceremonies by which they hoped to propitiate their deities, and that likewise they expected some reward for doing what they supposed pleasing to the same, and feared punishment for non-compliance with their wishes.

So far, then, some sort of religion is natural to man. He constantly feels his inability to cope with the difficulties which everywhere and at all times beset and assail him; and in his helplessness he turns towards the Author of things to ask for aid and enlargement. But if we examine into the opinions of past ages and of many nations of the present era, we shall discover that they were and are the most varied and contradictory. Some invest one alone with supreme power, while others deem two necessary to account for the origin of things, and others a multitude, more or less numerous, according to the system which they profess. Then, as regards duties, we shall be struck with the same variety; ceremonies the most distant from each other, worship the most strange to our views, means of propitiation the most contradictory, have been practised by intelligent no less than barbaric nations, and all in the hope of obtaining the favour of their gods or averting their wrath. Next, with respect to the rewards they expected and the punishments they dreaded, the same state of things will be observed: uncertainty and doubt are everywhere prevalent, a reasonable amount of certainty nowhere.

If, now, religion is natural to man, if he even should, in truth, be impelled to invent one to gratify his inward craving for higher things than his everyday life affords him: it would be, at best, a wavering, unsteady guide to which he would have to intrust himself, a fleeting and doubtful happiness which he could hope to attain, while he would be equally uncertain whether, after all, he had discovered any means to satisfy the gods whom he dreads, not loves. He might, also, in his ignorance of what the gods require, offend them when doing what he imagines would gratify them; and thus his acts of worship would prove injurious to him, and prevent his reaching the very object he sincerely aimed at to attain. Besides, where do we discover aught in nature to tell us precisely what the Deity is? did the great philosophers of Greece, such as Anaxagoras, Pythagoras, Socrates, Plato, and others, obtain anything like certainty in this great idea underlying all religions? did they ever rise to the sublime conception we have of God, who created all from nothing,—who spoke, and all came forth at his bidding? Go and look into the history of the gods of the ancients, or what is commonly known as mythology, and you will discover that everything animate and inanimate had its god or tutelary divinity; there was a god of fire, and one of the sea, one of the heavens, and another for the luminary of the day; fountains and trees were supposed to be watched over by the demons to whom they were assigned; while the passions also, both the virtuous and the vicious, were typified as superior powers or gods. I will not recite the names of the heathen idols in this house dedicated to the glory of the true God; but all of you can readily find them in the books which speak of them, and many are familiar to you already in your past experience. But this is uncontrovertible, that a uniformity of conception of the Divine Power is nowhere to be met with among the ancient and modern heathen; and, in short, their gods were the embodiments of their own gross natures, and they never rose with their deities beyond the conception of their own impulses and inclinations, as far as the popular belief, at least, was concerned. This being the case, their religion, such as it was, never could render them moral and virtuous, or, at best, it could not be the foundation of a uniform code of moral duties; and, without investigating the social condition of the heathen states, and determining how far they were inferior or otherwise to modern ones, we may maintain that any claim they had to moral excellence was not owing to their ideas of the gods, nor to any precepts which they could have received through their agency.

As to the views the ancients had of reward and punishment, such as they are represented by the poets, both Greek and Roman, who were doubtless, in a great degree, the religious authorities of the masses, a simple inspection will convince any one that the whole was merely a material thing; and, moreover, that the wrath of the gods was excited by trifling acts and thoughtless words, and manifested in a manner not reflecting honour on the vengeful beings who employed their superior power to afflict helpless mortals. We need not explain how little such a crude conception of responsibility, which could not fix on the probable act which might displease any particular inhabitant of Olympus, or whatever the fabled residence of the divinities might be called, could operate in checking the evil passions of man; since nothing a mortal might do could screen him from the malevolence or spite of some of the many worshipped beings, which all demanded homage, could all cause pain and suffering, and still differed in their opinions regarding what the son of earth should do to propitiate them.

The philosophers, such as Socrates and Cicero, no doubt had a more elevated conception of the preternatural world, and they also endeavoured to introduce a better moral system than the priests and their assistants could proclaim; but they, after all, could not prevent a thorough corruption, nor reduce the grossness of the conception under which the masses laboured. They only proved, living as they did centuries apart, that natural religion, notwithstanding that its truths are apparent at first sight, is not a safe nor a uniform guide, and is constantly liable to sink into corruption through the agency of designing men acting on the credulity of the people, who may be deluded and thereby brought under the control, both political and moral, of wicked designs, notwithstanding their advanced state of civilization; for no one can dispute that, in material greatness, Egypt, Assyria, Greece, and Rome, had made advances which modern nations have scarcely excelled, and of which the remains constantly discovered and explored furnish a striking evidence. What then is the pre-eminent claim of eternal or necessary truths? for, granting both their cogency and necessity, they are subject to the defects just laid before you.

If, however, the light of revelation comes to the aid of our reason, how marvellously accurate becomes our knowledge of things otherwise concealed from us! Instead of groping about in utter darkness to discover a god, we are at once informed that, before aught existed, there existed in all perfection the Eternal uncreated Lord of all, from whom all has sprung. His existence cannot be defined by us or to us,—our limited reason is not capable to comprehend his being from eternity, nor to define his duration, from any means of comparison at our command. But as regards his essence, we are informed that He is One, alone in his power, unaided in his government. Human reason, in examining the great diversity of animated and inanimated beings, was led to assume a diversity in the godhead (שתי רשיות or שתפות), or that antagonistic powers produce the varying effects of good and evil, mercy and punishment, which we observe. But our revelation tells us that all the effects we behold, both in the external and moral world, are the results of one Will, the products of one Mind, whom we call, for distinction's sake, by the various appellations given to Him in different languages, such as אלהים in Hebrew, *Deus* in Latin, *Gott* in German, *God* in English, which terms, though they sound differently, signify the same Being, who, moreover, to designate him from other gods, the products of human invention, is styled in his word אלהי ישראל "the God of Israel," as the national Deity, if we may so say, of the people that He selected as the bearers of his law. Instead, also, of our being permitted to imagine Him capricious, cruel, or revengeful, we are informed of his attributes, by which He is glorified, that He is "powerful, merciful, gracious, long-suffering, and abundant in beneficence and truth, yet not heedless of the acts of man, but punishing with justice, and never forgetting any deed of righteousness, while forgiving iniquity, and transgression, and sin, when forgiveness and pardon contribute more to the happiness of his creatures than severity and rigorous retribution." We therefore do not know Him merely by negative definitions, as some learned men have asserted, but He is represented to us by his positive qualities, termed the divine attributes, and they are such as to challenge the homage of all, and to impress them with the conviction, that One so great and infinitely good is alone entitled to the worship of his creatures.—So also as regards the duties we are bound to observe, and the acts which we should avoid in order to obtain the favour of this infinite God, we are not left to conjecture, by which we might be led in our ignorance to do the very things which would call down on us his condemnation and ill-will; but we are made sure that we shall act correctly, if we only follow the path which He has pointed out to us in his written law, a part of which was communicated to the whole assembled people of Israel, while the other portion was given through the intermediate agency of the man Moses, whom the nation of Israel selected as their messenger, pledging themselves to observe all that God might command him with respect to them. This law, so bestowed, was made accessible to all, it was written down in a code which has been preserved for all time; and thus our people have always had a sure and safe guide to lead them on the path of duty, which has been shown to be the second requisite for religion, since, without duties to fulfil, no faith can be imagined to have any existence.—And, lastly, with respect to the third element,—accountability,—Revelation has also placed this beyond the realms of doubt. In all the written records of God's communing with man, it is always prominently held up to him as a warning and incentive, that no deed escapes the cognizance of the Lord, who is ever ready to punish, and that no act of righteousness is forgotten amid all the transactions of the world, and will be recompensed according to its merit. Farther, we are told that no lapse of time or concealment will screen the sinner; and the whole tenor of the revealed law also impresses upon us the doctrine of the immortality of the soul, and, consequently, that the responsibility of man does not cease with this life; wherefore should he on earth be permitted to remain unscathed, he has by this means not escaped from the just visitation which his deeds have merited. It would take us too far from our subject to exhibit to-day the proofs of this doctrine, though I may briefly state that many Scriptural passages could not be understood, unless they meant to teach us that the spirit will be held liable in another existence for the deeds done in the flesh, so that the grave is no refuge for evil-doers. Thus also teaches Ezekiel (xvii. 4): הנפש החטאת היא תמות "The soul which sinneth alone shall die;" and thus was it taught to Adam in the beginning, when he was forbidden to eat of the tree of knowledge, "On the day thou eatest thereof thou shalt surely die," which, as he did not perish on the very day of the transgression, must mean that the accountability to be thereby incurred would be recompensed at a time subsequent in any state of existence; and thus we are likewise informed (Numbers xv. 30): "And that person shall be cut off from among his people," referring to one who daringly despises the precepts of the Lord.

We have, accordingly, in the scheme of revelation which is in our possession, all the requirements of natural religion which human reason might have imperfectly evolved by slow advances, while we have obtained them, perfect and precise, without a cloud of obscurity, and have thereby an infallible means, first, to know that there is a God; secondly, to know that there is a moral guide invariable in its principles, and where to find it; and thirdly, to feel that we are constantly under the cognizance and watchfulness of the great Being, who will, in justice and mercy, mete out punishment and reward for our acts, by an unerring measure of right, without prejudice or partiality, and guided solely by the welfare of all his creatures. It is thus that revelation has completed for us and all the world, if it will receive its instruction, what human reason had otherwise but dimly discerned and elaborated with insurmountable difficulties, without, after all, arriving at a satisfactory conclusion. It was, therefore, not perhaps necessary, as a deep thinker* of our race has maintained, for God to *reveal his existence* when He gave the Ten Commandments, where-

---

* Mendelssohn, in his Jerusalem.

fore he asserts that they were not needed to impart eternal truths, but merely a law or a code, which the legislation of Sinai confessedly is; but, at the same time, it was needed to rid mankind of the erroneous notions concerning God, the law, and responsibility; and to effect this it was well becoming the dignity of the Almighty to descend in his glory on the summit of Horeb, and there proclaim words of truth and power which were to rend asunder, and this forever, the vail which obscured human reason, and to teach to all the attributes which are his, and to proclaim his unity and eternity, his being the Creator and Ruler of all things, that He is the same from the beginning, and will be the same till time shall be no more.

But we must leave this part of our subject, and hasten to the one I intended chiefly to illustrate today, namely, *revealed* truths, in contradistinction to those termed eternal or necessary ones. While the latter are, as said, requisite as the basis of all religion, the first named are, on the contrary, only true because they are founded on the divine revelation in our possession. They could have been otherwise, or not at all, if God had so declared it to be his will; but having taught us that so or so it should be, we are bound to receive it, as emanating from the Source of all truth. If, for instance, the Most High had instructed us concerning the outcasts or dispersed of Israel, that they should be scattered over all the countries and never be restored, or in case He had said nothing concerning this point, we would be, in the first instance, authorized to assume that the dispersion of Israel was final, and that they would never return, any more than the day that is past will come back to us again; and in the second, we would be at liberty to indulge in conjecture, and assume whatever we might deem the more probable or agreeable theory. Restoration in either case could not be supported by Scripture, and, therefore, be no doctrine of Judaism. But on inspecting the Bible, we shall discover that it is emphatically and clearly taught there, that a time will come when the scattered remnants of Israel shall be restored to their ancient home, under the leadership of a chosen ruler and messenger of the Lord, the God of Israel; consequently, as those who have confidence in the One who has revealed himself by the light of nature and his spoken word, we are bound to put faith in this assertion and adopt it as a revealed truth, not necessary, indeed, as a prerequisite for Judaism, demanded for its existence, but as an imparted truth; wherefore it is a portion of its dogmas which we have received from the One, who cannot err himself nor deceive others.

On a previous occasion I have dwelt at length on the first part of the Haphtorah of to-day, contained in Ezekiel xxxvii., and exhibited to you the future union of the formerly hostile divisions of Israel and Judah, there represented as Joseph, the father of Ephraim, from which tribe the first king of the divided realm was descended, and Judah, as the leading tribe of the other division, from which the royal house of David also sprung. The future reunion of these parts was typified by the two sticks the prophet held in his hand being exhibited as one, or as some think, becoming miraculously joined together. At present I will refer merely to the subsequent portion, which is in these words (21–25): "And speak unto them, Thus hath said the Lord Eternal, Behold, I will take the children of Israel from among the nations whither they are gone, and I will gather them from every side and bring them unto their own land; and I will make them into one nation in the land, on the mountains of Israel; and one king shall be to them all for king; and they shall not be any more two nations, nor shall they at any time be divided into two kingdoms any more; neither shall they defile themselves any more with their idols, and with their detestable things, and with all their transgressions; but I will save them out of all their dwelling-places, wherein they have sinned, and I will cleanse them; and they shall be unto me for a people, and I will be unto them for a God. And my servant David shall be king over them, and one shepherd shall be for them all; and in my ordinances shall they walk, and my statutes shall they observe, and do them. And they shall dwell in the land that I have given unto my servant, unto Jacob, wherein your fathers have dwelt; and they shall dwell therein, they and their children, and their children's children forever; and David, my servant, shall be prince unto them forever." Here it is not declared that the separation and dispersion of Israel should be permanent; but, on the contrary, that a united people should be brought again to occupy their former country, which is clearly and pointedly described, and cannot be mistaken for any other. We cannot admit that the prediction of Ezekiel was fulfilled in the return from the Babylonian exile; for if you examine the books of Ezra and Nehemiah, you will find the whole number of those who accompanied Zerubbabel was forty-two thousand three hundred and sixty, and, if we add the few brought over by Ezra, the whole will be so small that no intelligent mind can maintain that the great and general restoration was thus accomplished. Moreover, prince David is promised as the future ruler of the returned Hebrew nation; but, again, the history of the world does not give us any trace of this being accomplished; for as yet no governor of the ancient line of our kings bears sway in any part of the world, certainly not in the land which our forefathers possessed, where we are strangers and servants, as it is this day. The only excuse men can frame for refusing to believe this prediction is, that so great a length of time has elapsed since it was uttered, that its accomplishment appears doubtful and uncertain. But here again we must refer back to the Authority who gave the inspiration. It is God our Creator; He declared that the future should thus shape itself, at a period not made known to us, but which He reserves to himself to hasten or to retard, according as the world may be prepared for it; and who can therefore tell Him that He has forgotten what He promised, or delays unduly the accomplishment of his word? It is, therefore, our duty, as the receivers of the divine revelation, to continue steadfast at our post, and hope on and forever, till the time when the words of prediction shall become facts realized in the history of man, as they surely will be; because the One who uttered them is of infinite power and truth, and who speaks not a word which returns without fulfilling its mission.

There are, however, some of Israel who assert that our dispersion was for the benefit of the world. The legislation on Sinai was calculated only for an exclusive people; it was separated by prohibitory laws from the rest of mankind, and its isolation in Palestine was still more calculated to keep it apart from others. But when it ceased to be a nation, when its political union was severed by the conquering arm of Rome, it received a new mission. It was sent with this into the world at large, and it has fulfilled its task by making the word of God known everywhere, by scattering universally the blessed principles of love and mercy, and giving thus the impulse to the high civilization which the diffusion of the Scriptures will effect. Those new teachers who argue after this fashion, while seemingly giving the greatest weight to the principles and power of the Bible, deny at the same time the evident meaning of the words employed. To them restored Israel means a world brought under the dominion of the Divine Word by the progress of enlightenment and civilization; the prince David, or the scion of David, or the sprout from the root of Jessé, is neither more nor less than that the Hebrews in their scattered state shall, as messengers of divine truths and by their mere presence, unite the whole world in the worship of the true God, and thus carry the great principle, which was confided to them in their state of isolation, to all sons of men, after their national bond was dissolved for the purpose of making them truly priests and teachers of the Most High. The language of prophecy is then farther interpreted to signify that by this means peace shall be made universal; that is, that the diffusion of knowledge is to produce what the words of the Bible apply to a single agent, who is generally termed the

Messiah. Practically, there must result from this view, as far as Israelites are concerned, that we should not expect a personal redeemer, nor a national restoration; but that we must be content with the only redemption which awaits us in common with all the world, the prevalence of a universal acknowledgment of the one God, by which means the redemption of mankind from error, barbarity, war, and servitude shall be effected.

I will not detain you too long, nor fatigue you by elaborate arguments to confute this assumption, which is certainly not warranted by the plain words of the Bible; but I will merely ask those who teach after this fashion for the smallest particle of proof, which could convince us that their hopes of a universal acceptance of the true idea of God can be accomplished in the manner in which the events of history follow each other now. Go whither you may, you hear the cries of the defeated and the shouts of the victor; chains are unloosed here to be fastened there on the limbs of others; crimes are prevalent everywhere, and justice seems almost to have fled from the earth. And let the advocates of the new doctrine enter into any of the churches, cathedrals, chapels, meeting-houses, or by whatever name the various places of religious assembly are called, whether in this powerful and highly educated country of America, or in enlightened England, or civilized France, or intelligent Germany, or mighty Russia, or smiling Italy, or any other land where the religion of the Nazarene is professed, and they will not hear the name of the One Eternal invoked. He is not honoured in their assemblies; but they will find that, in

Protestant countries, the son whom they allege to have proceeded from God the father, has usurped the honours due to the last, and in Catholic lands it will be discovered, what is still worse, that the reputed mother of the son, the associate god, has claimed all reverence and worship, and is invoked as the immaculate intercessor with the divinity for the transgressions of sinful man. Where is there in all this the slightest evidence that the theory (I will not speak aught of the practice) of our faith is progressing among the men whom we live? Or is it better among the Mussulmans, or the heathen races, among whom our remnants are also scattered? During a period dating back eighteen centuries, we have been teachers by word and deed, have protested by our presence against the errors of dogma and worship of the rest of mankind,—and we are this day still alone in our adherence to the One Eternal. Multitudes of gods, stocks, and stones, are adored by the Pagans; horrible phantasies are worshipped by others of a lower grade; in other lands the prophet of Mecca has his followers, who place him high above our teacher, and fancy to find in his book a more sacred record than our Scriptures; and among our neighbours they have an associate in the work of the government and salvation of the world,—and in a few days they will celebrate the birth of this associate in the divinity, as though the uncreated God, who existed from eternity, could be born of woman, and be afflicted with the fallible and failing nature of mortal man.

If the progress is onward, and of this there is no doubt, it is still very slow, and no one is wise enough to fix the period when it will reach the point which a philanthropic philosophy desires to attain. No cosmopolitan exposition of the Scriptures can guide us here, although it may be averred that all men are, equally with Israel, objects of care to the Almighty. We, however, who have been taught by God the truths concerning himself and what He has given us as the expression of his will, cannot reasonably hesitate to adopt in full the belief in the promises He has made for the future, and to confide sincerely in their fulfilment in the manner indicated in the Bible, just as we adopt with a sincere conviction the eternal truths of which our reason had an indistinct perception, and which revelation has rendered clear and intelligible to all understandings. It is not for us to say that God's method for the world's education is unreasonable, or that we will not bear that part which has been allotted to us in this glorious work. It may be painful for us to follow out the path assigned to us; but we only accomplish our mission by persevering, and leaving the issue in the hands of our Master, who will not fail to employ the proper instruments to reach the proposed end. How glorious were, therefore, the faithful of our race, who, in all ages, looked upon the outward world as a mere shadow that is passing away, while the truth they had been destined to defend was never to perish, but to become victorious after all! They beheld, indeed, the nations of the earth established in the seat of power; they saw them enjoying pleasure and ease, even while these blasphemed the name of the Most High. Yet while they suffered, yet while they breathed forth their pure souls amidst tortures and violence, they beheld the bright future unveiled before them, and they saw the brow of Moriah crowned again with the sanctuary of the Lord, and his glory filling the holy place; they saw the people assembled to the worship of the One and Holy, and nations streaming to the open portals of God's house to learn wisdom and knowledge from the faithful shepherd whom the Lord will raise up to spread peace and truth on earth,—and they died resigned to the decree which called them hence, glorifying the One who had specially selected them as an acceptable sacrifice needed for the accomplishment of the words of promise to Israel and to mankind. And though many stakes were kindled to burn the bodies of the saints, and though many scaffolds were stained with the blood of fearless martyrs, let us not imagine that their sufferings were in vain. Their ashes will ever be piled up as a memorial before the presence of the Lord, and not a drop of their blood has been drunk up by the earth to be forgotten; but it will fructify the soil of truth, it will enrich the field of God's sacred law, and cause it to bear abundant fruit for the day when the Lord shall be revealed before the eyes of all flesh, when they will all submit to his faith, and shall bear voluntarily the yoke of the heavenly kingdom. On that day shall the hopes of the pious of all ages be fulfilled, and then shall idols be hurled from their bases, false worship shall be banished forever, and the Lord shall be One and his name One. Amen.

DISCOURSE XIV.*

DIVINE CHARGES.

Brethren and Friends!

Having been requested by your president, after the conclusion of the service yesterday morning, to address you this day on the concerns of our religion, I did not consider myself at liberty to decline, although it being a holy day, it has been out of my power to sketch even the subject on which it is my intention to speak.—You know that we claim to be a people selected by God to uphold the religion which He promulgated to us on the festival of Pentecost, the second day of which we now celebrate, and in our prayers we return thanks to the Lord for this selection, in the following words:

אתה בחרתנו מכל העמים אהבת אותנו ורצית בנו
ורוממתנו מכל הלשונות וגו' :

"Thou hast chosen us from all people; Thou hast loved us, and favoured us, and exalted us above all the nations, and sanctified us with thy commandments, and brought us near to thy service, O our King! and hast called us by thy great and holy Name."

---

* This and those following to the end of the volume are written out from memory. Some of my sermons left a particularly strong impression on my mind, and the substance has, therefore, not been forgotten, though I do not pretend to be able to recall the very words I used. This one was delivered in the (New York) Shearith Israel Synagogue, on the second day of Pentecost, 5614.

Christians and unbelievers assert that we are vain boasters for so thinking and speaking; that we certainly have no superiority over others, on the contrary, are inferior, the ones say, in religiousness and devotion, the others in intellectuality, as these fancy to believe that all acquiescence in positive religion is an evidence of a deficiency of intellect. We, indeed, should not concern ourselves much about what enemies to all religion may say or think about us, nor about what those who interpret the Scriptures, as our Nazarene neighbours do, may advance concerning the correctness of our belief. But it is a very different matter as regards their strictures about our evident religious conduct; for herein they are right that it does not authorize us to boast of any superiority on our part. It is too notorious that, however pure and holy our principles are, our conformity to duty is lamentably deficient; and let us say what we will, the world can only judge of the excellence of any principles by the fruit, or outward practice which they produce. But how does it look among us in this respect? Cast your eyes around you, friends, in this very holiday, dedicated to the service of God, on this day, which, in addition to its being observed in commemoration of the giving of the Law on Sinai, is also the Sabbath, the sign of the everlasting covenant between God and Israel. But why are so many seats vacant on this solemn day? What is the cause that those who should occupy them are not among us to worship the Lord? Then go to what you call here "down town," and you will find the merchant busy in an endeavour to sell his wares, and to collect in his debts; the broker and banker striving at their desks to obtain the gain of their absorbing pursuits, and the mechanic industriously engaged in carrying on his handicraft or supervising his manufactory; but all alike sedulous to increase their store, without inquiring whether this is the day and this the hour when worldly work is to be pursued, whereas it is the day and it is the hour when all should be assembled as one race to do honour to the Lord and King of Israel, who is the Author of life and the One who in his pleasure blesses our labour. It is deplorable that so many of Israel do not seem to understand the real value of the various pursuits in which we spend our lives. We must indeed toil to procure what we need for our sustenance and that of our families; there is need for employment to give vigour to body and mind, which both deteriorate under slothfulness and habitual idleness. But we ought not to forget, that it is equally absurd, equally pernicious, to force Heaven, as it were, to give us success, to bestow on us wealth. Were it that we could live honourably only through unremittent toil, the Lord would not have given us Sabbaths for rest, and festive seasons for rejoicing. The Scriptures would have thundered in our ears the primitive curse addressed to Adam, "In the sweat of thy face shalt thou eat bread;" they would have enjoined us, "Toil incessantly, labour unremittingly, struggle ceaselessly, till you return to the earth from which you were taken." But this is not the language of our eternal Benefactor; He wanted to break the chains of toil, to loosen the bonds of labour; and hence He gave us the weekly day of rest, that the weary may find repose, that the exhausted may recover his strength, to exert a renewed vigour for renewed exertion. And He has told us, moreover, that the Sabbath is his rest, a day devoted to Him because He is the Creator of the universe, consequently able and willing to bestow on us on the sixth day his blessing, that we may then have all twofold bread, as compared with the preceding days, so that we may not have need to gather food on the seventh, the period of our weekly divinely-appointed rest. The violation of this command proves conclusively that we have no confidence in the co-operation of the Lord with our work; wherefore we can claim no superiority in consequence of our election, while we exhibit ourselves just as the children of the world, whom no conscience restrains, who only yield to the fear of being coerced by the police-laws of the land, before they will consent to refrain from their avocations.

The neglect of the precepts which we have received to distinguish us from all people, the non-observance of the festivals which have been bestowed on us as memorials of our departure from Egypt, at once stamp us, in the eyes of our neighbours, as unbelievers in the very faith we pretend to revere, and no professions of ours, however loudly uttered, will remove the impression of our outward conduct. The gentile, therefore, who, though erroneously, adheres to a divided godhead, who rejects as obsolete the commandments of Moses, who ignores the seventh-day Sabbath, the Day of Atonement, and the festivals, who eats what he alleges his creed permits him to eat, has a superiority over us, who profess to believe the contrary of all he confides in; since at least he is consistent; he has convinced himself that his premises are correct, and his belief and conduct simply correspond thereto. But how is it with the Israelite, who, let us assume, initiates his first-born in the covenant of Abraham, on the Lord's day of rest, (whereas the sealing of the babe with the token of the eternal bond, and the prayers recited, in fact, acknowledged the eternity of the circumcision and the Sabbath as an ordinance which cannot be moved while the laws of heaven and earth continue,)—when the sacred act is passed hastens to his week-day occupation, as though he had lost time while engaged in the service of his Maker? He has indeed conformed outwardly to the duty which Israel expects at his hands, the Sabbath has been sanctified, in name, within the walls of his dwelling; but he has delivered by his subsequent conduct a false testimony against God and his faith; he has said emphatically that he submits to a burden which public opinion, or an affectionate wife may demand of him to assume; but his heart is elsewhere, it is wedded to his idols of gold and of silver, and that Judaism has no real hold on his conviction. You can amplify this example, brethren, for other cases; and frame what excuses you may, invent reasons of necessity or expediency, and the case remains unaltered, the transgression brings odium on his own brothers, and gives the enemies of Israel ample opportunity to search our character, and to cast suspicion on the sacredness and eternity of the Law proclaimed from Sinai. We, however, were selected and endowed with the best of knowledge, "In order that all the people of the earth might know that the Lord is God, and there is none else." We were preserved during a long course of centuries to preach, by our presence, that we mean to uphold for all time the law and testimony, to confide in none but the Sole Eternal, and to be guided by no other statutes than those which He delivered to us from the midst of the fire. If then we are blasphemous in our conversation, if we are heedless in our conduct, we tell our heavenly Father that we wish not to have any inheritance in his house, that we are unwilling to be numbered among his servants. Thus acting we are not elevated among the nations, nor called by the Lord's holy Name, who emphatically promised us, "In every place where I will permit thee to mention my name will I come and bless thee." If you then do not come to the house where He is adored, if you rely on your own labour for success, if you imagine that your own wisdom will counsel you aright: you at once exclude yourselves from a claim to divine aid and support; complain not, therefore, if your toil bears no fruit, if your wisdom should fail to discover the path which leads to success. If you should be afflicted with sickness after you have not invoked Him when in health, you will not have any right to expect consolation from on High to assuage your suffering, and to be supported by his spirit on the couch of sorrow.

But, Israelites! whether you honour the divine Wisdom which chose you as a people endowed with wise laws and just statutes; whether you are willing to conserve in your persons the precepts and ordinances which form the body of our system,—they are nevertheless true, and will vindicate their vitality after you and others who rebel against the Lord have ceased to be on earth. The Code promulgated through

Moses was not given to perish, nor were Abraham's seed chosen to be blotted out from the face of the earth. The word was to be believed in forever; the messenger of the happiest tidings ever conveyed to mankind was to be the trusted prophet for all times; and happy will it be for each and all of us, were we to strive to regulate our conduct not by the appeals of interest, not by the persuasion of sinners, not allured by the false spirit of the age which essays to place human reason in the stead of the holy Scriptures, and labours persistently to rend the bond of union which connects us with the past, which strains every nerve to tear apart the chain which binds us to the distant future, when it will be made clear to all that our selection was a reality, our elevation an undisputed fact; when we shall wear the crown of glory instead of an aggrieved spirit, and everlasting joy shall dwell on our heads, when all mankind shall adore with us the One who spoke audibly to our fathers, and said to them that they should be to Him a peculiar treasure, because He is the proprietor of all the earth, and can therefore rule uncircumscribed, without any one to gainsay his will, or arrest his power.

You should consider farther, brethren! that in this city are assembled the largest number of Israelites of any in America, and that almost daily new accessions are made by immigration from Europe. Much depends on the religious tone which prevails here, and on the general reputation you have in the community among those who do not profess our faith. Little value as some may attach to this latter consideration, it is of great weight nevertheless. All new-comers do not come hither penniless; all who arrive here do not belong to the uneducated classes. But it is precisely this which you ought to ponder on deeply. Do not show the new-comers from abroad that you have no higher reputation than successful merchants, or perhaps to speak more correctly, lucky traders. Let them not see that, for instance, you who belong to the oldest, and I may say a body excelled in respectability by no other in this land, are ambitious only to be known as those who do and can live in fine houses, wear elegant clothes, fare sumptuously and indulge freely in all pleasures and ornaments. For, let me admonish you, the evil will be contagious; the vain conceit of young men and women of a European worldly education will counsel them to shun such society, and to seek, while concealing from all their ancestral faith, the company of those who excel you in true respectability and importance in the community. You know yourselves that in a wealthy city like this, where riches have been hereditary for several centuries in the same families, who have acquired gradually a degree of refinement which the possession of ample means can secure to its possessors by obtaining and imparting the highest attainments in science, literature, and arts, no mere acquisition of the amplest fortune will open for you, for any man, that mysterious circle "good society." It needs the key of merit, of mental elevation, of an unblemished character, to unlock the chains which clasp it; and I see no reason why Israelites should not, if they will, be numbered among the leading men of New York who stand foremost for princely charity, and who encourage every enterprise for the diffusion of literature and the promotion of their religion. There are many of your neighbours, who would consider themselves disgraced by acting openly against the practices which they hold sacred. Why then not take example by them? be wealthy and religious, be rich and enlightened, be worldly great and worthy of Heaven? So acting as I hinted, you will gradually establish a healthy Jewish religious opinion; you will almost compel all strangers to join your circle; for the moment it would be discovered that they were traitors to our cause through false shame, they would be repudiated by those whom they endeavoured to deceive regarding their origin and true opinion, for I hold it superfluous to prove that an instructed Hebrew can only believe sincerely in his faith, no matter how often he has been washed by the water of uncleanness, and how often he has forsworn the God of Israel.

Independently, however, of all considerations, more than for yourselves, more than for Israel, more than for the world at large, more than for the sojourner who comes among us, be concerned for the children whom God has bestowed on you. When you neglect their religious education, they never can become intelligent in the faith; when you teach them preëminently secular knowledge, the science of Judaism must remain to them a sealed book. When you despise your fellow-Israelites, and permit them not to become welcome visitors in your houses, you will imbue them with a silly contempt for those whose friendship they ought to cherish, and from among whom your sons and daughters are in duty bound to choose, at their maturity, wives and husbands. If you merely teach them religion by rote, engage ever so many instructors, who perhaps follow their often unpleasant calling, owing to the stupidity or perverseness of your spoiled offspring, slovenly and listlessly, you have not accomplished anything in training them properly, while you, parents, are heedless of the ways of truth, neglect its precepts, and show in all your actions that you are devotees to gain and pleasure, accumulating in one instance to heap up useless riches, or in the other to squander them in ostentatious expenditures and useless extravagance. Do you love your children? does your heart throb, mothers! for those you reared from infancy? Yes, I know the father will shield his son from the winter's blast, fold him in his warm embrace, though exposing himself almost to certain death. If the son were on a narrow plank overspanning a deep chasm, though the first step would almost to a certainty hurl the frail bridge into the boiling gulf below, he would see nothing but the one to whom his soul was bound, and hasten to his rescue, not listening to the warning of danger, nor to the earnest appeals to desist from the mad attempt. If your daughter, youthful mother! should be cast on the bed of sickness, consumed by a violent and contagious fever, though even the physician you send for says that all hopes of recovery are vain: will you listen to the counsels of prudence, and abandon your beautiful, your only hope to the care of hired nurses, who are inured to infection, and fear no malady? I need not wait for your answer, you would scorn the advice of prudence, you would refuse to believe in the opinion of the leech; you would insist to watch yourself at the side of the tiny crib; no sleep would weigh down your eyelids, no fatigue would benumb your limbs, and you would wrestle in prayer with your

Physician above to spare you this agony, to cause this cup to pass away from your lips; and not till the last breath be drawn, or till a merciful God has sent his angel of recovery and assuaged the fever and strengthened the feeble limbs, will you go to your chamber in the consciousness that you have discharged your duty, and that no neglect can be laid to your account, and that you yielded not to hired strangers what you could do better than they from natural impulses, and motives of maternal affection. Now, parents! if you are so anxious to prove yourselves worthy of the beautiful part confided to you, if you feel the full obligation resting on you as those who have an interest above all others in those who have sprung from you; if the physical life is of so great value, that you will risk your own to save that of son and daughter: why will you be less careful of their spiritual existence, which should be at least equally dear with the other? You perhaps imagine the children are yours—yours to dispose of them as you may deem proper, for your gratification, for their aggrandizement! But you are mistaken, they are not your property, they are *God's charges*, intrusted to you for awhile to render them by your exertions best fitted for his kingdom. What will you answer, when your disembodied spirits appear before his judgment-seat, and He addresses you in the awful voice of his indignation: "What have you done with MY children? Why have you permitted my son to become a blasphemer? Why have you suffered my child to forswear the law which I have given you as an inheritance for all your generations forever? Why have you by neglect allowed my daughter to join the assembly of the stranger, when you by early chiding, by timely reproof, by setting a good example, could easily have retained her a faithful member of the congregation of Jacob?" What can you say, that you were too busy to watch their course, that it was no more than right that they should enjoy the wealth for which you had toiled, that the spirit of the time prevented you from insisting on strict conformity? that it could not be expected that your well-born and highly cultivated daughter should seek for a mate among the neglected and humble sons of Israel? Will this avert the doom which you justly deserve for having neglected God's charges, for not being able to return them unto his keeping when He demands them back at your hands?

Reflect well on this, parents! it is the most serious thought that can occupy your mind; children are yours for a time, to be a blessing to you, and to enliven the household. But after all they are only lent, intrusted for awhile to your keeping, to fulfil on and through them the precepts which God has given us: "Teach them—the words of the Law—diligently to your children, speaking of them when thou sittest in thy house, when thou walkest by the way, when thou liest down and when thou risest up." Let the religion not be a banished subject, but a household word, of which all shall know the purport, and with which all shall be familiar. Have the emblems of our faith constantly about your dwellings, let the pious and intelligent of our people be welcome in your family-circle, also then when you display your wealth and hospitality by inviting numerous guests to your mansion. Accompany them to the house of God, and accept no frivolous excuse for their absence; and above all, expose them not to temptation by heedless indulgences, by which their virtue and piety could be gradually undermined. In brief, act in this respect as you would in the case of bodily contagion; and see to it, that should a sinful course have been entered on despite of your instruction, warning, and example, you exert all your energies to arrest the evil, so that, if moral recovery or moral death ensue, you cannot accuse yourself that you have been the means that a precious soul has been lost to Israel.

In this manner should we celebrate our festivals, that they may be remembrancers to us of our whole duty, incentives to deserve the respect of man, the favour of God, and the approbation of our conscience; and that we may sincerely say and feel, that the Lord has greatly blessed us in selecting us to be the bearers of his law, and to be his witnesses on earth, that He alone is the Creator who spoke audibly his omnipotent will to our fathers when they stood at the foot of Sinai.

DISCOURSE XV.

OUR STRONG CITY.*

BRETHREN!

As you have, by the act of dedicating this hall to the service of the God of Israel, taken your station as a distinctive body among the great family of Jacob, it is proper that we reflect on what has been accomplished. Till a few months back you were attached to another house of worship, which is still large enough to receive all who now are about to assemble here in their daily and weekly devotions. Yet you left, because you felt no longer at home in your ancient dwelling, and you have opened this building, of far less extent in space and inferior in beauty, in order to meet here to accomplish your religious duties. So let us investigate the object of the synagogue, and connect with it a reflection on our religion, as an emblem of which it is established. For our text we will take Isaiah xxvi. 1, 2.

ביום ההוא יושר השיר הזה בארץ יהודה עיר עז
לנו ישועה ישית חומות וחל: פתחו שערים ויבא גוי
צדיק שמר אמונים:

---

* In consequence of an attempt to introduce modern reforms in the old Bnai Israel congregation of Cincinnati, a new community, bearing the name of Shearith Israel, was founded in the beginning of 5616, and having fitted up a synagogue, which was dedicated on Sabbath Vayakhel, 29th of February of that year, I was invited to deliver the dedication sermon, which I complied with, as above.

"On that day shall this song be sung in the land of Judah, A strong city have we; his aid will He grant us as walls and defence. Open ye the gates, that there may enter in the righteous nation, that guardeth the truth."

Our religion is indeed a strong city, and by the Lord's gracious assistance it is furnished with ramparts, towers, and walls. On these He has placed the sons of Israel as watchmen and defenders; they are not to be slothful in vigilance, nor negligent in warding off the danger. For before the enemy has yet assaulted our city, should the watchman proclaim aloud that he is approaching, and all who hear the call should be ready to hasten forward to ward off the evil which might produce destruction to the cause of God and his people. It is indeed, therefore, a momentous work which you have just completed. For, though the habitation of the Lord is the entire universe, which exists only in Him, you have devoted this place as his dwelling, among others established in Israel. But why? Because you felt that you were expelled, by the majority of your former associates, from participating farther in their communion. Mere human reason would, under no circumstances, influence us with the wish to erect a special house of assembly; for why confine the divine presence within the narrow limits of a structure raised by human hands? You, however, relied on the written word of God, which permits us, nay, orders us, to make Him a sanctuary, in order that He may dwell among us. Still, how is He to dwell among us? was not the temple twice destroyed? did He not give over his own residence to the power of the unbeliever, who shouted forth his notes of triumph as though he had overcome the power of the Most High? why was the fire kindled, which could not be quenched till all that was destructible had fallen a prey to the flames? It was the sinning of Israel which caused all this; it was the backsliding of those who ought to have been sincere worshippers in the sacred precincts which destroyed their sanctity; nothing but the outward shell was left to the adversary on which to wreak his vengeance; but the presence of the Lord had long since fled, it was no longer his dwelling, no longer acceptable, no longer needed, and therefore it fell, and with it the people who had sinned; and thus they who had contemned the words of the prophets, learnt by sad experience, that mere outward worship, lip-service, is an abomination to the God of truth, who requires the heart and spirit to be united in his adoration. A place of worship for Israel must have something more than beauty and spaciousness to sanctify it, something far more than psalmody, and music, and oratory, to dedicate it as an acceptable offering to the Most High: it is the complete surrendering of our will to his will, the subjecting of our inclinations to his commands, the yielding of our entire selves to his guidance, which alone can effect this; and with this every place where we assemble in his Name will become a centre whence blessings will be diffused far and near; for God will be there to sanctify what we undertake, to complete what we commence.

The body of Israelites with whom you were hitherto connected, are large and respectable; for this reason, therefore, there was no motive for your separation from them; the synagogue, for which you contributed for many years your means to support it properly, is both ample and beautiful; it was natural that you should feel a deep attachment for the structure where you had spent so many hours of devotion, where you so often experienced the joy of a sincere period of religious reunion, on those solemn days when all assemble, as one man, to do honour to Israel's King. Nor were you bidden by your associates to quit them; you might have stayed among them, and accepted the rules they would establish, and the new form of worship they may introduce, and the modern doctrines they purpose holding up as that which the Jew is hereafter to follow. Yet you felt that you could not submit to this consistently with the character of true believers, and seeing that the majority was against you, and likely to increase in process of time, you regarded the late proceedings of your fellow-members tantamount to a decree of expulsion, unless you would submit to what you justly conceived unbecoming your religious character. Therefore you quitted the old synagogue, because you feared the march of innovation, which here, as elsewhere, threatens to spread dissension and unbelief in our ranks, and to uproot the ancient system of belief and practice, which has become endeared to us by ages of suffering. For what was it against which priests, nobles, peoples, and kings conspired, as we may justly call it, during so many centuries of agony which passed over our head? was it not against the observance of the Sabbath and circumcision? was it not our belief in one God? was it not against our teachers? was it not against our law and the books in which it is treasured up? If we had yielded, as so many of us did in the hour of trial, we might have dwelt in peace, "eaten up by the land of our enemies," as the great teacher says in his awful denunciation of punishment for our transgression (Levit. xxvi. 38); for if we wished not to do needful battle for our and God's cause, why should we not disappear from the earth, as so many nations of antiquity have done? what was to be conserved, if not our law? yet how could we exist without it? It was this the rulers of the world understood fully as well as we; and therefore they strove to make our days bitter, and render our life a burden to us. But the more fierce grew the persecution, the narrower appeared the field on which we could move: the more intense grew our devotion to the divine legacy, the more confirmed became our devotion. Thus though we were fearfully diminished in numbers, though banished from what we fain regarded as our homes, though turned out naked and famishing upon the wide world: we still saved, as our imperishable inheritance, the law of Moses, which had been confided to us for safekeeping, and it is ours at this day. Our constancy, however, at length wearied out the spirit of hostility of our opponents, who clearly saw that the finger of God was in our preservation, who never suffered us to be banished at once from all countries, and opened up for us always an asylum, where we might rest awhile to recover from the rapine and slaughter, and to be refreshed with new strength; and they learned by degrees to treat us more kindly, and not to hunt down the sons of Israel "like a partridge on the mountains." And now we have a time of respite; whether our peace is to last forever or not is more than I will venture to say; but at least now we are unmolested in many countries, and we can practise our religious duties without supervision or restraint on the part of the civil authorities. But the usual results of ease are already visible among us, and now men have arisen who endeavour to place a new construction upon our ancestral religion, and strive to rob us of our hopes for the future, which ever cheered us on in the seasons of the deepest gloom, and caused us to look with the confidence of a future triumph for our principles, in the Lord's own good time, over the puny though mighty efforts of vain and presumptuous men. These leaders seem to forget that our sunshine may continue only for awhile; in days of comparative ease, it is possible then, we might be able to sustain ourselves simply as a sect which has its members scattered everywhere, held together by a community of certain principles and practices, more or less valued and adhered to. But this even is doubtful, it is as yet an untried experiment. We always regarded ourselves, and were so looked upon by the world, as a nation or a people, in the words of David, וכי כעמך ישראל גוי אחד בארץ "And who is like thy people, one nation on the earth," &c. (2 Sam. vii. 23.) If therefore dispersed, if our sins plucked us through the children of iniquity out of our own land and home, we never yielded the idea of one nationality; nay, believed in the promise of God that the scattered elements would be gathered together, and the land be restored to its rightful owners, to whose labour alone it will yield its increase, who shall possess it forever, without an enemy to molest them, without a warlike host to consume the products of their regenerated soil, and fields and vineyards restored to the ability of giving their increase, just as the nation of

Israel itself shall be by repentance and righteousness restored to the favour and grace of their eternal King. —But destroy this expectation, wipe out the glorious predictions which our prophets recorded on our behalf, or what is the same thing, if we permit our modern teachers, who desire to break down the bridge which connects the present with the past and the future: is there not every danger that the people, bereft of the idea of a coming unity, may at length give up the struggle against the assaults of the opinions of the world, and become insensibly uncircumcised in heart no less than uncircumcised in flesh? Behold, brethren, all religious opinions are now, and have been for more than a hundred years, subjected to a severe criticism; men, who are called philosophers and naturalists, have endeavoured to deny the whole system of revelation; and though thousands of able men have risen to defend the general truths enunciated by the Bible, the traces of the conflict are plainly visible in the councils of our neighbours; the authority of priests has greatly waned, and many people no longer receive the dicta of the church with the same implicit yieldingness as heretofore. It is possible indeed, that the issue of the conflict will ultimately be, that men may resort to Jewish interpretation and instruction, thinking truly that the absurdities and contradictions which disfigure the opinions of Nazarenes and Mahomedans are not chargeable to our faith. But this very result, should it occur, would be the period of the greatest jeopardy for Israel, if we are without the firmest faith in our future reunion. For, if we should see millions willing to come to us, to be with us one people, on the sole condition that we should yield our ceremonial observances, giving them and retaining for ourselves simply the great characteristic of our faith, the *belief in the Unity*, and declare the moral law alone permanent: who sees not that this would be a virtual extinction of Israel's identity? Can it be possible that the Almighty caused us to pass through fire and water, through tribulations which no other race of men ever endured, simply that a period of peace should quietly and resistlessly effect what no force nor combination of powers could ever accomplish? It seems to me, that to a correctly reasoning mind, the answer is too evident to require any elucidation farther than the simple statement just presented to you; and we need not envy the intellectual capacity of that man, who would endeavour to prove that amalgamation with the world is all right if we ourselves are the willing agents, and wrong when those who divide the dominion of the earth among them demand this by the force of civil and ecclesiastical authority.

But there is another danger, namely: the calm now prevailing may one day cease again. Education, enlightenment, and progress assume very often strange phases; the hatred of the Jew, at least of his religion, is a dormant feeling in all churchmen of whatever kind, and neither Nazarene nor Mahomedan, as a class, has ever shown an undivided and sincere attachment to our faith. Suppose then, this present state of religious dissension, which is so wide-spread that its existence cannot be denied, should suddenly or gradually terminate; that parties now hostile to each other, seeing that they mutually destroy each other's interest and influence, should conclude a hollow truce, pretend hypocritically that their differences are all reconciled, and then make common cause against us by exceptionable legislation or social exclusion, which in many respects is even more efficacious: what would our condition be, if we had done what is now demanded of us, on pain of being branded as unenlightened, stripped ourselves of distinctive observances and hopes, and left only an imperceptibly narrow line between us and the gentiles? As it is, we see constantly men of intellect, without any other motive than base interest, or the hopes of rising in political life, even in this country, forming alliances with gentile families to escape the odium of even the faintest, the most attenuated Judaism; in Europe, our opponents boast that the greatest minds who occupy the chairs of instruction in the universities were once called Israelites; judges, ministers of state, officers in armies and navies, have for the sake of position thrown off their connexion with the household of Jacob; and it requires no spirit of prophecy to foresee the increased danger of annihilation to our people, if we break down all "the walls and defences" which the help of God has erected for us.

You have thought that you saw symptoms of this danger in the innovations which have been proposed among your former associates; you conceived, not without good reasons, that many were becoming unfaithful to their trust; and knowing after making proper efforts that you would be left in a minority, and outvoted on questions of the greatest moment, which, by the by, let me remark, are not in the province of any congregation to discuss, much less to decide upon, you have done the next best thing, to withdraw from a community which has become in a measure estranged, or threatens to do so for itself, from our ancestral customs, and to conserve in your new organization the ancient landmarks which our fathers have set for us. At the same time, I know that the act of severance must be painful to all of you. You have laboured hitherto conjointly with your late associates for the advancement of our cause; many of you were here before the new synagogue *B'nai Israel* was erected, when a mere handful of Jews laid the foundation of the now flourishing body which still worships in a neighbouring street; you had a common burial-place, where the dead of your several families repose quietly in peaceful graves; there, are interred your fathers and mothers, your wives and husbands, your sons and daughters, your brothers and sisters. But this place of sepulchre is no longer yours, for in quitting your associates, you have yielded the right of property to all that the community possesses together; when your summons therefore comes, you cannot expect that your ashes will mingle with the dust of those you cherish in the recesses of your memory, for the line of separation has been drawn no less between those who yet live and are active on the face of the earth, than those who are departed, whose time of action is past. No, it was no cause for joy that you came hither to dedicate this hall to the service of God. It was well therefore that you did not enter here with the sound of harp and drum,* with the voice of the flute and trumpet, nor with the melodious psalm-

---

* The dedication service was of the simplest kind, and only a few verses of Psalm cxviii. were chaunted by a volunteer choir.

ody and pleasant music; you came hither in serious earnestness, like exiles who were driven from their own home by the resistless force of outward power. It would have ill become you to exhibit tokens of outward joy; but you acted wisely and religiously in entering these doors with the serious reflection of men who have taken a step, the full responsibility of which they recognize, and depositing the books of the law in their proper receptacle, that they may be a testimony against you, lest you do not faithfully adhere hereafter to those principles for which you have organized the community known as "the Remnant of Israel." You had a higher object than triumphing over your brothers; it was the cause of our faith which induced you to quit them, and you have entered these portals as "a righteous people that guardeth the truth," in the words of our text, that truth which Israel, as a people, has received from its ancestors.

It has become habitual of late years among certain persons to sneer at old-fashioned or orthodox Jews as they are now nicknamed, as those who favour ignorance among the masses, and are the enemies of scientific improvements. It is true, unfortunately, that many who have studied in universities have forsaken the ancient standard, while those who were not so contaminated by the wisdom of the gentiles have remained faithful. But, brothers, it is not true for all that, that all who have studied sciences have become faithless. Look at the host of brilliant lights who now illuminate the horizon of our German native land, and who are also scattered in other countries, and yet are found steadfast among those who guard the faith and truth of Israel, and you will have no cause to blush for these champions on the score of a ripened intellect, extensive erudition, vast practical knowledge, known as they are in all the walks of science, wielding the pen of the ready writer, with eloquence second to few of their calling among other persuasions. It is deplorable that so many became fainthearted and sought for fame and profit in the camp of the stranger; but let us not admit for a moment that true enlightenment is incompatible with the strictest adherence to the belief and practices of our ancestors. Be not ashamed of the defenders of our faith, they are worthy of it, they are worthy of Israel; and though the unthinking multitude may be at times misled by the pretentious appeals of the seducers, who flatter their vanity in order to confirm them in sin, though you see many faithless whom you suppose ought to be as faithful as you : stand firmly to your post, and remain unshaken, although few only are left to guard with you the strong city of the Lord. This is indeed an age of trial; our shackles have just been removed from our limbs; our enemies, who formerly closed against us all avenues of elegant arts and sciences, seeing that thus we would cling only the closer to our sanctuary, have opened for us high-schools and universities, and bidden us to enter to quench our inappeasable thirst for knowledge. They knew that our soul longed once more to dip into the fountain of science, the access to which had been so long interdicted to us. Many hastened thither to drink before their soul had been fortified by wise instruction, and had learned to distrust the appeals of a deceitful world. When their studies were completed, and they came forth decked with academic laurels, they were told that for the Jew there was no employment in the state, this is Nazarene, and none who denied a divided godhead could be paid for public services. The weak and the timid fell, and they are now reckoned among the enemies of Israel; the firm expatriated themselves into countries where the Hebrew's talents can be available without a change of faith, while others laboured and do so to this day in inferior positions, much less than their talents could justly lay claim to, and labour for the welfare of their own brothers. That there are many also who climbed the ladder of knowledge, only to become scoffers, is, alas! too true to be denied. But is this the only sinning generation? were we not in Isaiah's time a people laden with iniquity? Yet did the faith not perish, and it survived as you all know the wreck of state and temple-worship, the cessation of priesthood and kingdom. No, brothers! orthodoxy is not the friend of darkness, it demands universal education, that all may know the duties they owe to their God, and the deeds they should perform towards their fellow-men. That all claiming affinity with us are not enlightened, pious, liberal, truthful, is indeed to be deplored; but have any class ever been perfect? Therefore do you endeavour to set a holy example to all; endeavour to promote a system of healthy education among you, that all of you may be from knowledge followers of ancient Judaism, sincere followers from conviction of the God of Israel. You are all watchmen in the city of the Lord; He has helped you thus far; take heed that the ramparts and walls be not left undefended, and see to it that when these gates open, those who enter it may be ready no less to guard the truth from all foreign admixture, and prepared to conserve the faith of Israel all the days of their life.

May then the blessing of our Father rest on you all, in order that He may perfect the work you have begun, that peace may dwell among you, and righteousness flourish through your exertion, so that it may be well with you all the days. Amen.

DISCOURSE XVI.*

THE 'OMER.

Is this not a beautiful day? Look out! The sun is shining clearly with the mild rays of spring, and sends not down the scorching beams which compel us in the summer to seek a shelter against his oppressive heat. Everything invites us to go abroad and enjoy the balmy spring. Behold, the earth has been awakened out of her winter's sleep, she has thrown off the torpor of the icy season; the fresh green grass once more springs up at the call of the change of season, and flowers again dot the landscape. The herds and flocks once more can venture out on the pasture, and receive their food directly from the bountiful hand of our heavenly Ruler, without waiting for the intervention of man. The birds come home again from

---

* Delivered at the Synagogue Beth El Emeth on the second day of Passover either of 5618 or 19.

their winter's journey, and seek their old leafy bowers, or the cliffs and banks where they build their nests. And man too again seizes the tools of agriculture, to procure himself food and sustenance from the ever open, ever yielding bosom of the soil, and he looks with joyful anticipation to a bountiful harvest, to crown his annual labour with success. The day is indeed beautiful, a bright spring-day when all feel relieved in the thought that the cold winter has passed away.

Yet do we not wander abroad in the field to enjoy awakened nature, and why? we felt ourselves called upon to enter our house of worship in accordance with the customs of our fathers, to celebrate this second day of the festival of our redemption from Egypt. To the true Israelite there is a higher duty than to enjoy the pleasures of this life; he must not pluck the roses as they bloom, nor call a day misspent on which he has not tasted the cup of joy. For if this were all for which we are to exist here, how many would be defrauded of their just claims to pleasure; unless you would assume that the earth and its fulness were created for the rich and indolent who, without working, without contributing the least to the general prosperity by their exertions, who produce nothing and consume the fruits of others' labour, can obtain in indolence all they need, looking with pity and contempt on all who produce what contributes to their ease and comfort. We cannot so accuse our eternal Father. It is well that in his judgment there should be those who have ample means to purchase the labour of others; but they are responsible for the use of their leisure time, for the hours of their relaxation as much as any son of toil. There is enough to be done by the children of affluence, if they will employ their time to their own advantage and the promotion of the general welfare; there is no need of their hunting constantly the phantom pleasure, and deceitful enjoyment; and just in proportion as they solve the problem which their position has imposed on them, will they be benefactors of their fellows, or injurious to the peace of society. That so many fail in this, is only another proof that man is apt to mistake the apparent for the real good; just as those whose condition calls on them to struggle for their daily bread, often fall into habits of slothfulness, and become useless to their families and a burden to society at large. All classes of men should take heed that they fulfil what their duties demand of them; and then will they have no cause to accuse the All-just for having neglected them, especially in the distribution of his manifold gifts among the sons of man.

With these remarks prefaced let us consider a portion of the law-section which we have read this day. "When ye shall have come into the land which I give unto you and reap the harvest thereof: then shall ye bring an 'omer full of the first of your harvest unto the priest. And neither bread, nor parched corn, nor green ears, shall ye eat, until the self-same day, until ye have brought the offering of your God." And the text thus continues:

וספרתם לכם ממחרת השבת מיום הביאכם את עמר התנופה שבע שבתות תמימת תהיינה : —
והקרבתם הנחה חדשה לה' :

" And ye shall count unto you from the morrow after the holy day, from the day that ye bring the 'omer of the wave-offering, that it be seven complete weeks—and ye shall then offer a new meat-offering unto the Lord." Levit. xxiii. 10–16.

I have condensed the passage, selecting the main points, which refer to our subject. The feast of Passover was in Palestine the commencement of the barley-harvest, this being the first grain that ripens there. It might have been in early seasons which occur at times, that a man's field was ripe before the feast; if now he were of right permitted to use what is his as he pleases, he might have cut his grain, and prepared it in the manner indicated in the Scriptures, which was no doubt the custom of the country, and enjoyed what his land had produced for him. But the commandment steps in between him and his inclination, and tells him that until the people had, through their delegates, brought a small portion of the new harvest to the sanctuary, no one should presume to call an ear his own; not until Israel had annually acknowledged that the increase of the soil was in very truth the Lord's, who graciously permitted them to partake of his bounty, should a mortal claim the right to dispose of what otherwise may be his own. And why? You can easily frame the answer. It was to teach us that we are responsible for the use of our means to a higher Source than man; that we should not say, We have laboured, we have succeeded, and the fruits of our toil are justly our own. For this was the doctrine of Judaism : namely, that we are mere stewards on earth, to hold our possessions at the will and disposal of the Grantor of our prosperity, and that hence it may be resumed justly, should we transgress the conditions of our tenure, and disregard the restrictions which have been imposed on us. It was thus that the wealthiest in Israel, nay the chief of the state, could not anticipate, while he obeyed the law, the period when all might partake of the earth's products, and thus all were practically taught that wealth and possessions were not absolute property, but only held for the advantage of all who are like them the sons of faith, and children of the same parentage.

But after thus introducing the cycle of the annual festivals, that period especially which marks the time between the redemption and the promulgation of the law, a peculiar commandment was given us to number actually the forty-nine days which elapse between these periods, and to note the fiftieth especially as a day of a renewed offering to the Lord. Let us attempt an illustration. We may assume the Passover to be the period of our early manhood, when the age of childhood and youth are already past by. In infancy we scarcely heed the days as they glide past. They are bedecked with sunshine or overcast by evanescent clouds. Few indeed remember the age of childhood, seldom an hour thereof is impressed on the memory. So also when the youth prepares himself for his calling, he is under the tutelage of parents, or guardians, or those in whose charge he may be placed, and happy will it be for him if he is judiciously guided, carefully controlled, and wisely instructed. So was our education as a people in Egypt. We went thither in the boyhood so to say of our nationality, and in the iron furnace of affliction we were taught to look up to our eternal Saviour for enlargement, as all the gods of men's invention are helpless themselves, without power to withstand the Almighty's fiat. This our redemption proved. The stubborn will of Egypt's people and king had to yield before the outstretched arm of the Most High, and He led us forth with joy, that we should not be any more the slaves of man, but servants to our Redeemer. Our youth and its struggles were ended, and the period of our tutelage was overpast, when the hosts of the Lord were led forth with a high hand, as the Scriptures call it, by his chosen messenger.

As it is with nations, so it is with individuals; when the age of irresponsibility is over, that of independence and its accompanying accountability commence. We cannot fix the precise date when this eventful change takes place in us; but the Bible has assigned the twentieth year as the one when the Israelite, after having at his thirteenth year entered into his individual responsibility to his Maker, became a full member of the state, bound to go out with the armed host of his countrymen to defend the soil against invasion, whether the assailants were many or few. No one could be exempted from this patriotic duty, except those who, elsewhere (Deut. xx. 5–8), were excused by public proclamation from participating in the conflict. But in point of fact all Israelites having equal rights had equal duties; and no one could devolve on another the right which his home and his country had on the valour of his arms. The Psalmist says, that our days on earth are seventy years, and rarely reach eighty; experience proves the correctness of this ancient statement, and when we reach the verge of threescore and ten, we lose the elasticity of our steps, the vigour of our limbs; the light of our eyes is dimmed, nay our intellect, perhaps, becomes uncertain and vague, and those on whose advice nations depended, those who moved public assemblies by their fervent eloquence, the poets who charmed multitudes by the sweetness of their numbers, musicians whose tuneful strains have become the delight of the world, are now only shadows of their former selves, and they linger perchance awhile longer on the stage of life, to be soon and inevitably gathered to the home destined for all the living. The picture is sad and depressing; it is what awaits us all; we cannot avoid the pangs of disease nor the terror of dissolution; they tower up before us in the dim though sure distance, and neither craven fear nor daring indifference can ward off what

[The proof down to this word was sent to Mr. Leeser on December 28th, 1867, but he never recovered sufficient strength to complete the writing of the sermon. A few days after the receipt of the proof he wrote on it the following, which he intended for the printer. It was found among his papers after his death: "I tried yesterday to write, and succeeded in jotting down about twenty lines; but I find I must wait a little longer. There shall be no useless delay. I feel easier, but suffer greatly.
L."

The twenty lines alluded to have not been found.]

www.ingramcontent.com/pod-product-compliance
Lightning Source LLC
Chambersburg PA
CBHW032148230426
43672CB00011B/2483